MW00469879

Rationalism, Empiricism, and Pragmatism

AN INTRODUCTION

Consulting Editor

V. C. CHAPPELL
The University of Chicago

Rationalism, Empiricism, and Pragmatism

AN INTRODUCTION

by Bruce Aune

UNIVERSITY OF
MASSACHUSETTS
AT AMHERST

McGraw-Hill, Inc.

New York   St. Louis   San Francisco   Auckland   Bogotá
Caracas   Lisbon   London   Madrid   Mexico   Milan
Montreal   New Delhi   Paris   San Juan   Singapore
Sydney   Tokyo   Toronto

RATIONALISM, EMPIRICISM, AND PRAGMATISM: AN INTRODUCTION

COPYRIGHT © 1970 BY McGRAW-HILL, INC.
ALL RIGHTS RESERVED. PRINTED IN THE UNITED STATES OF AMERICA.
EXCEPT AS PERMITTED UNDER THE UNITED STATES COPYRIGHT ACT OF 1976,
NO PART OF THIS PUBLICATION MAY BE REPRODUCED OR DISTRIBUTED IN ANY FORM
OR BY ANY MEANS, OR STORED IN A DATA BASE OR RETRIEVAL SYSTEM, WITHOUT
THE PRIOR WRITTEN PERMISSION OF THE PUBLISHER.

Library of Congress Catalog Card Number: 72–102088

MANUFACTURED IN THE UNITED STATES OF AMERICA,
BY THE COLONIAL PRESS INC., CLINTON, MASS.

5 6 7 8 9 DOHDOH 9 8 7 6 5 4 3 2 1
ISBN 0–07–553543–2

DESIGNED BY WILMA ROBIN

To Herbert Feigl

Preface

This book was written for use in undergraduate courses in the problems of philosophy. A common means of organizing such courses is to concentrate on some of the main problems of metaphysics, ethics, and the theory of knowledge. This book is designed to provide a thorough treatment of basic issues in the theory of knowledge. It may be appropriately combined with the instructor's favorite texts in metaphysics and ethics.

Although elementary discussions of the theory of knowledge normally mention the traditional controversy between rationalists and empiricists, they rarely have much to say about pragmatists. This may have been justified at certain times, but it is no longer acceptable when philosophers as influential as Nelson Goodman and W. V. O. Quine are emphasizing their commitment to pragmatic principles. I have accordingly done my best to offer today's student at least an elementary understanding of this increasingly celebrated approach to knowledge. In addition, I have made a special effort to improve upon the usual skimpy treatment of the old dispute between rationalists and empiricists. The usual treatment is skimpy because rationalism tends to be quickly brushed off as an obviously misguided position whose significance is chiefly historical. Anyone intimately familiar with recent contributions to the theory of knowledge is well aware, however, of the current vitality of rationalist principles. It is really not much of an exaggeration to say that rationalism, like both empiricism and pragmatism, is as alive today as it ever was.

My strategy in writing this book has been to present a clear, sympathetic account of each of these three distinctive theories of knowledge, emphasizing the basic considerations that have led, and still lead, very shrewd, sophisticated thinkers to accept them. Since I am convinced that the student profits greatly from studying the actual words of classic philosophers, I have enriched my exposition with long extracts from the writings of Descartes and Hume. I had originally planned to include similar extracts from the work of C. S. Peirce in my discussion of pragmatism, but I was dissuaded from this by the exceptional difficulty of his writing. My concern throughout has been to make my discussion maximally comprehensive yet fully understandable to the undergraduate, who in many of our universities must unfortunately compete with more than a hundred other students for his instructor's attention.

In the past decade or so, various techniques of critical analysis have become popular with teachers of philosophy. I have had very little to say about such techniques in this book. My aim has been to present a reasonably dispassionate survey of standard objections and replies to important issues, leaving it to the instructor to introduce the critical techniques he happens to favor. I have tried but doubtless failed to keep my own philosophical biases discretely in the background; yet I hope my presentation of these opposing theories of knowledge is still sufficiently fair so that my book will be useful to instructors whose philosophical sympathies differ sharply from mine.

A final note of caution. This book is really intended to be what I say it is, an elementary treatment of a field of philosophy. Sophisticated readers will no doubt find many points of oversimplification and will be tempted to object that certain positions are excessively idealized. I make no apology for such simplifications and idealizations in an introductory book. My purpose will have been achieved if the student gains a solid understanding of fundamental issues and has only a minimum to unlearn in more advanced courses on the subject.

Special thanks are due to two of my colleagues: Joe W. Swanson offered useful comments on Chapter IV and Larry Foster helped me to clarify some of the ideas set down in Chapter V.

B. A.

Contents

Rationalism, Empiricism, and Pragmatism

CHAPTER 1

Descartes and Rationalism

The technical name for the theory of knowledge is "epistemology," which is derived from the Greek *episteme*, meaning "knowledge," and the suffix *ology*, meaning "science of." In its original sense the word "science" meant "an organized body of knowledge." What we now call "theory of knowledge" is fully in line with these etymological facts, for it purports to be, or to create, an organized body of knowledge about knowledge. This is without doubt a peculiar subject, and a word about its origins will therefore be helpful.

1. Why a Theory of Knowledge?

According to Aristotle, knowledge began from wonder, and the earliest thinkers we regard as philosophers certainly wondered about the nature of knowledge and formulated numerous theories concerning it. An interest in knowledge itself, as opposed to special kinds of knowledge such as mathematics or physics, is easily generated when accepted teachings about fundamental matters begin to seem doubtful or unconvincing. The ancient Greek philosophers experienced this kind of doubt, and in their efforts to resolve it they were led to reflect on the ultimate nature of knowledge and to invent in the process the subject of epistemology.

An important source of doubt for these ancient thinkers concerned the origin and nature of the world. Traditional teachings on this subject were replete with what we now call myth; they described the birth of Chaos and Earth, the emergence of the gods, and the creation of men. In breaking away from this mythic picture and in thinking out an alternative in something like a scientific spirit, these early thinkers were led to the conclusion that the world is really very different from what it appears to be. This opened the door to serious disputes about the true nature of reality, and in their turn these disputes generated extended controversy about the nature of knowledge itself.

According to Heraclitus (c. 540–470 B.C.), the world is a thoroughly dynamic system (a "fiery flux") in which permanence and stability are something of an illusion. As reported in Plato's dialogue *Cratylus*: "Heraclitus . . . says that everything moves on and that nothing is at rest; and, comparing existing things to the flow of a river, he says that you cannot step into the same river twice."[1] Such a view of the world is not only surprising, but it raises the crucial question "How do we *know* that reality differs in this way from the so-called appearances we are said to observe?" Heraclitus did not answer this question explicitly, at least as far as we know. Instead, he emphasized the extreme difficulty of knowing true reality ("Nature loves to hide") and stressed the ignorance and stupidity of his fellows ("It is not characteristic of men to be intelligent").[2]

A contemporary of Heraclitus, named Parmenides, did try to explain how reality is known, but he ended up with a view that was even more surprising than Heraclitus'. According to Parmenides, "thought and reality are the same": whatever we can think must be so, for what is not so is not, and what is not can neither be said nor thought. This view might seem to imply that every stupid remark ever made is actually true, but it really has the opposite effect: most things "said" are really false. His major line of reasoning was this. Whatever is, is; and whatever is not, is not. Since to say, as Heraclitus did, that reality is not ultimately stable is to say that something is not, such a statement must be false; for it implies that what is (reality) actually is not (not stable). As Parmenides saw it, Heraclitus was completely wrong in thinking that change even exists, let alone dominates reality. If a thing changes from being A to being B, it must, when A, be not-B; and it must, when B, be not-A. But since what-is-not is not, a supposed change involving not-B or not-A is clearly impossible. Hence, change cannot occur.

Parmenides' view of reality seemed as bizarre to his contemporaries as it seems to us today, but the logic behind it was not at that time easy to refute. A later thinker, Protagoras, turned his back on the idea that there is an ultimate reality lurking behind appearances and argued that our knowledge concerns appearances and nothing else. In one of Plato's dialogues, *Theaetetus*, Protagoras is described as holding that "man is the measure of all things"—so that things are to one man as they appear to him and are to another man as they appear to him. When a wind blows on two men, feeling hot to one and cool to the other, we can say that the wind *is* hot to the one and *is* cool to the other; for each man is the measure of all things—"of things that are, that they are; and of things that are not, that they are not."

Protagoras' evident relativism about the facts of nature was extended to include standards of behavior. Different societies have different standards of behavior, and what seems right to one society is right for it, while what seems right to another society is right for that one too. There is simply no objective truth holding for all men regardless of how things may seem to them and no objective standard of right and wrong that is binding on all men regardless of the societies in which they live.

Protagoras' relativistic view of moral and natural knowledge seemed completely false to Plato. As he saw it, one cannot reasonably claim that all knowledge is relative because in doing so one implies that some of it is not, namely, the knowledge one claims to have. To allow that the latter knowledge may also be relative is completely self-defeating, since it will also allow the alternative claim of Heraclitus and Parmenides that genuine knowledge is never relative. If we are to avoid an out-and-out contradiction, we must therefore grant, Plato thought, that at least some knowledge is nonrelative. But if we do this, we must then admit that there is such a thing as absolute truth about which men may be right or wrong. This will leave us with the task of determining when they are right and when they are wrong—the task, in other words, of determining what claims to knowledge are objectively true and what claims are objectively false.

For Plato, Heraclitus and Parmenides were undoubtedly correct in thinking that knowledge is nonrelative and concerns the true (rather than the apparent) nature of reality. In developing his views Plato made use of the leading ideas of both men. Following Heraclitus, he held that the natural world is in constant, thorough-going change; but like Parmenides he held that true knowledge must concern something unchanging and eternal. Taking geometry as his paradigm of genuine knowledge, he argued that what we really know are ideal objects such as triangularity, circularity, and number. Unlike things in nature, these ideal objects can be fully understood and precisely defined. No circle drawn in the sand is perfectly circular with a circumference of exactly $2\pi r$. Things in nature merely approximate the shapes we can know mathematically, and for this reason our opinions about them are at best "likely stories."

In addition to admitting ideal mathematical objects as things of which we may have genuine knowledge, Plato also admitted ethical objects (he called them Ideas or Forms) as genuinely knowable as well. Examples of such objects are Courage, Temperance, Piety, and Goodness. These ethical ideals are also eternal and unchanging, and are capable of exact understanding. Unlike these Ideas, a man's behavior is only approximately understandable. No man is perfectly good or perfectly pious; no man acts in a perfectly courageous way. The ethical qualities of human beings are always matters of degree: one may be more or less courageous, but not perfectly so. This lack of human perfection makes genuine knowledge of human beings strictly impossible. We can know what Courage is, and we may observe that a man's action is courageous to a certain degree. But because the action is, at best, an approximation to the ideal of Courage, our understanding of it is also only an approximation to ideal understanding or genuine knowledge. Like circles drawn in the sand, human beings are only partially understandable, and our considered views about them are at best "likely stories."

Strange as his views may seem, Plato was so influential for subsequent thinkers that a famous twentieth-century philosopher was led to say: "The safest general characterization of the European philosophical tradition is that it consists of a series of footnotes to Plato."[3] Plato's idea that true knowledge is restricted to a domain of ideal objects and that things in nature are understandable only approximately is, in any case, merely an example of the many astonishing ideas regarding man and the world that philosophers have developed throughout history. Other philosophers have insisted that man is really an immaterial spirit lodged only temporarily in a body; that the world is simply an artifact produced by a designing God, who loves (or, as some say, is indifferent to) the men He has created; that evil, like space, time, and change, is an illusion; that each man has a definite place in nature and society that should not be changed; that the universe is (or is not) a fully deterministic system allowing no possibility of genuinely free human actions; and so on.

In view of this wide range of important philosophical claims about man and the world, it is obviously important to have a secure means of evaluating their credentials; of determining which views are right, which are wrong, which are mere conjectures, which are probable, and the like. To be able to make such evaluations, one must clearly understand what knowledge truly is, or what it is best understood to be. Such understanding is exactly the goal of the theory of knowledge, and this is why the subject still exists and is important.

2. Descartes and His Mathematical Method

Although the entire history of philosophy is fascinating and worth careful study, we shall begin with the modern period and consider the attempt of a justly famous thinker to develop a theory of knowledge adequate to settle philosophical controversy once and for all. The thinker is René Descartes (1596–1650), commonly regarded as the father of modern philosophy. Apart from the intrinsic importance of his general theory of knowledge, his attitude, his approach, and his method make him a natural starting point for the contemporary student.

Descartes was greatly suspicious of past philosophy and even of what he had learned as a student in one of the finest schools of his day. Not only did he find it possible to doubt most of what he was taught about philosophy, but he could not accept the grounds on which much of it was based: the authority of learned men. This distrust of traditional authorities and standard opinions motivated his own distinctive approach to philosophy, which was to disregard traditional wisdom and to start from scratch, thinking out a philosophy in a completely fresh way. His method was to proceed in a mathematical fashion, first establishing his axioms or fundamental principles and then deriving consequences from them in the manner in which mathematical theorems are derived from mathematical axioms. By using the rigorous method of mathematical reasoning, he hoped to establish something lasting and definite in philosophy and to avoid the morass of futile controversy that seemed distinctive of the philosophy he had learned in school.

To employ the mathematical method in his philosophizing it was necessary for Descartes to isolate primitive truths corresponding to mathematical axioms. His strategy for accomplishing this was to adopt a procedure of systematic doubt. He would subject his beliefs to a systematic review and attempt to isolate those that he could not possibly doubt. Such indubitable beliefs could be regarded as absolutely certain and would therefore provide a suitable foundation on which to build his philosophy. In his words:*

> Many years ago I realized how many false opinions I had been accepting as true ever since my childhood, and how doubtful everything I had based on them must be. I therefore decided that if I wanted to establish anything solid and lasting in the sciences, I must deliberately rid myself of all the opinions I had hitherto accepted, and begin building again from the foundations. . . . It will not be necessary, for this purpose, to show that they are all false, a task which I might never finish; but since reason has already persuaded me that I ought to withhold belief no less carefully from things which are not entirely certain and indubitable than from those

---

* The following passage, and others indicated in the notes, are reprinted with permission from *Essential Works of Descartes,* translated by Lowell Bair. Copyright © by Bantam Books, Inc.

which appear to be manifestly false, the slightest grounds for doubt will be enough to make me reject any of my opinions. And for this I have no need to examine each one of them in particular, which would be an endless labor, but, since the destruction of the foundation brings about the collapse of the entire structure, I shall first attack the principles on which all my former beliefs are based.[4]

Descartes' aim is thus to seek indubitable truth by examining the foundations of his former beliefs. If, on examination, the basis for a group of beliefs can be doubted, then he will not regard those beliefs as entirely certain. Such beliefs may, of course, be true; but if their basis can be doubted, he will not claim certain knowledge of them. Perhaps later, when he has found absolute certainty, he may be able to come back to a rejected belief and show that it is true. But for the moment—for the immediate purpose of his systematic doubt—he will put it aside as untrustworthy.

Note that when Descartes speaks of doubting certain beliefs, he has in mind a *rational* form of doubt. A belief that can be rationally doubted is one that a careful thinker may find positive reason to suspect; grounds can be given for thinking that it might possibly be false. An indubitable belief, on the other hand, is one for which no doubt inciting reason can possibly be found; it is apprehended as absolutely certain.

Descartes proceeds:

Everything that I have hitherto accepted as truest and most certain has been learned either from the senses or through them. Now I have sometimes found the senses to be deceptive, and it is prudent never to place complete confidence in those who have once deceived us.

But although the senses sometimes deceive us with regard to very small or distant objects, there may be many other things which, even though they are known by means of the senses, cannot possibly be doubted, such as the fact that I am here, sitting by the fire, wearing a dressing gown, with this paper in my hands, and so on. How could I deny that these hands and this body are mine? To do so would be to liken myself to those madmen whose brains are so disturbed and clouded by dark bilious vapors that they persist in assuring us that they are kings when they are poverty-stricken, that they are dressed in purple when they are naked, that they have clay heads, that they are gourds, or that they are made of glass; but they are insane, and I would be no less demented if I were to follow their example.

However, I must bear in mind that I am a man, and therefore in the habit of sleeping, and that I imagine the same things in my dreams as these madmen imagine when they are awake, or sometimes even more absurd things. How often have I dreamed that I was here, fully dressed and sitting by the fire, when I was actually undressed and lying in bed! At this moment it certainly seems to me that my eyes are awake as I look at this paper, that the head I move is not asleep, that I am intentionally and deliberately extending this hand and feeling it. What happens in my dreams is not so distinct as all this. But I recall having been often deceived by similar illusions while I was asleep. When I reflect on this at greater length I see clearly that there are no certain indications which distinguish waking from sleeping, and I am so amazed by this that I can almost believe myself to be asleep.[5]

In the absence of any "certain indications" by which to distinguish waking from sleeping, Descartes allows it possible that his perceptions of moving his body, seeing paper, and so forth are mere illusions and that his body and the perceptible world around him may be quite different from what he takes them to be. Yet even if his senses are wholly deceptive, it occurs to him that he may nevertheless know many things that do not depend on sense perception, such as the fact that $2 + 3 = 5$, or that a square has no more than four sides. Whether he is asleep or awake, it does not seem possible that he could be deceived about truths of this simple, obvious kind.

But, on second thought, error may be possible in these cases, too. He has always believed in an all-powerful God, and a being of this awesome power could certainly have arranged matters so that Descartes is deceived in everything he thinks, including such apparently simple facts as that $2 + 3 = 5$. His belief in these matters is clearly due to his innate intellectual ability, and an all-powerful being could, no doubt, have affected his mind so that he falls into error whenever he tries to add two numbers or count the corners of a square.

It may be granted, of course, that the God he always believed in would not actually deceive him in this way, but an evil spirit might easily do so. As a means of adding rigor to his method of systematic doubt, Descartes finds it useful to suppose that an evil being of this kind exists. The method of doubt is in practice very difficult to employ, since old, habitual opinions constantly come to mind and almost dominate his belief against his will. The supposition that an evil genius, one as powerful as he is cunning and deceitful, is using his powers to deceive him will keep Descartes constantly on his guard against dubitable opinions, no matter how plausible and attractive they may appear. He therefore supposes that the earth, the sky, and in short all the external things we seem to perceive are only illusions produced by the evil genius; and he considers himself as really having no hands, no body, and no organs of sensation. These suppositions will so "arm his mind" against the evil genius that he will not assent to anything that is dubious or uncertain.⁶

Having prepared himself in this way to resist even the most subtle forms of deception, Descartes raises the question "What is there, then, that can be regarded as true?" The first answer that comes to mind is "Perhaps only this, that nothing is certain." But this answer is not obviously true. For all he knows, there might be numerous certainties that he has simply failed to consider. One question worth exploring is whether his current thoughts have a particular cause. Might they not have been produced in his mind by some other being, perhaps God or the evil genius? This does seem possible but it is obviously not certain, since he is perhaps capable of producing the thoughts himself. This last possibility suggests an important idea, however: If he were actually the cause of his own thoughts, he would certainly have to exist. But is not his own existence an utter certainty anyway? The fact seems undeniable; yet it is highly perplexing because he has already found reason to doubt that he has a body. If the existence of his body is in doubt, does it not follow that his existence is also in doubt? On reflection the answer seems to be "No."

If he is doubting, he must necessarily exist as a doubter, as a being who does the doubting. You cannot doubt if you do not exist. Since he is unquestionably doubting, he unquestionably exists; his existence is an utter certainty. This certainty cannot be shaken by the hypothesis of the evil genius, because Descartes cannot possibly be deceived about his own existence. If the genius succeeds in deceiving him about anything, he must nevertheless exist as a being who is deceived. You cannot be deceived if you do not exist; you cannot even think if you do not exist. Since he is clearly thinking at the present moment, his present existence is, for him, utterly indubitable, whether he actually has a body or not. He cannot err in concluding, therefore, that "the proposition, *I am, I exist*, is necessarily true each time I state or conceive it."[7]

Descartes has now discovered his first absolute certainty: He exists whenever he thinks, whenever he doubts, believes, or even conceives of something. But this knowledge is extremely limited in content. He knows that he exists whenever he thinks, but he does not know what he is. Great caution is therefore required at this stage of his meditations. He must be especially careful not to mistake something else for himself and so go astray in this knowledge that he maintains is "the most certain and evident of all."

Still supposing that there is a supremely powerful and malignant demon who employs his power and skill to deceive him, Descartes proceeds to consider what can be ascertained about his own nature as an existing thing. As we have seen, he cannot assert that he possesses a material body. Can he say that he has a faculty of sensation? Again the answer is "No." Nothing can be sensed without the use of a body, and Descartes has, in any case, often dreamed that he was sensing things when in fact he was not. Is his knowledge of his nature then limited to his mental activities? The answer is "Yes."

> Here I find what belongs to me. I am, I exist: that is certain. For how long? As long as I continue to think, for it might be that if I ceased to think, I would also cease to exist. I am not now admitting anything which is not necessarily true; I am therefore regarding myself only as a thinking thing, that is, a mind, soul, understanding or reason—terms whose meaning has hitherto been unknown to me. I am, then, a real thing, one that truly exists. But what kind of thing? I have already said it: a thinking thing. . . .[8]

To facilitate his search for further knowledge Descartes now attempts to identify the distinguishing features of an indubitable truth. He does this by attending carefully to the element of certain knowledge that he has just discovered. He finds that there is noth-ing to this element of knowledge but a "clear and distinct appre-hension" of what is affirmed; his certainty that he exists amounts to no more than a clear and distinct apprehension of his existence. Apprehension of this kind must, therefore, be a certain mark of truth; if he could ever go wrong in thus apprehending something, he could not be totally certain about his own existence. Accord-ingly, he adopts the general rule that whatever he apprehends very clearly and distinctly must be true.[9]

Although this general rule seems understandable in the light of his discussion, it involves two terms that have an important technical meaning in his philosophy: "clear apprehension" and "distinct apprehension." Descartes explains their meaning in *The Principles of Philosophy* (1644):

> I call that clear which is present and apparent to an attentive mind in the same way as we assert that we see objects clearly when, being present to the beholding eye, they operate upon it with sufficient strength. But the distinct is that which is so precise and different from all objects that it contains within itself nothing but what is clear.[10]

He amplifies this explanation by saying that when a severe pain is felt, the perception may be very clear and yet not distinct, since the pain (which exists in the soul) may be confused with "the obscure judgment" one might form of its nature—for instance, that it exists in a hand or leg.

The explanations just given do not fully clarify Descartes' diffi-cult notion of a distinct conception, however. His reflections on the nature of a piece of wax offer a much better idea of the dis-tinctions he wishes to draw. These important reflections also il-lustrate a point he will never abandon—namely, that sense-per-ception provides a very uncertain basis for genuine knowledge:

> Let us begin by considering those things which are commonly thought to be the most distinctly known, namely, the bodies which we touch and see. . . . Let us take, for example, this piece of wax which has just been taken from the hive. It has not yet lost the sweetness of the honey it contained; it still retains something of the odor of the flowers from which it was gathered; its color, shape and

size are visible; it is hard and cold; it can easily be touched; and it emits a sound when it is struck. In short, everything required to make a body known with the greatest distinctness is present in this one. But now, as I speak, it is moved near to the fire: what was left of its taste is dispelled, its odor vanishes, its color changes, its shape is lost, its size increases, it becomes liquid, it grows hot, so that it can scarcely be touched, and it no longer emits a sound when it is struck. Is it still the same wax despite these changes? We must admit that it is; no one can deny it, no one can think otherwise. Then what was there in it that was known so distinctly? It was certainly none of the properties that were perceived through the senses, for everything that was subject to taste, smell, sight, touch or hearing has been transformed; and yet the wax remains.

Perhaps the wax was what I now think it to be: not that sweetness of honey, or that pleasing odor of flowers, or that whiteness, or that shape, or that sound, but a body which appeared to me under a certain guise a short time ago, and now appears to me under another. But what, precisely, is it that I am now imagining? Let us consider the matter closely; let us see what remains of the wax after we have removed everything from it which does not belong to it. All that remains is something extended, flexible and malleable. But what is meant by "flexible" and "malleable"? Does it mean that I imagine that the wax can have a round shape, then become square, then triangular? By no means, for I conceive it as being capable of taking on an infinite number of shapes, and my imagination is incapable of encompassing this infinity, so my conception of the wax cannot have been produced by the faculty of imagination. And what is extension? Is it not also unknown? It becomes greater when the wax is melted, still greater when it boils, and continues to grow as the heat increases; and I would not be conceiving this wax with clarity and truth if I did not think that it is capable of more variations in extension than I have ever imagined. I must therefore admit that only my understanding, and not my imagination, can conceive what the wax is. I am speaking only of this piece of wax in particular, for what I say is still more evident with regard to wax in general. Now what is this wax which can be conceived only through the understanding, or the mind? It is certainly the same wax that I see, touch and imagine, in short, the same wax that I have been supposing it to be from the beginning. What must be particularly noted is that our apprehension of it is not an act of seeing, touching or imagining, although this may formerly have seemed to be the case, but an inspection of the mind which may be imperfect and confused, as it formerly was, or clear and distinct, as it is now, according as my attention is directed more or less closely to the constituents of the wax.[11]

Descartes began with a fairly clear perception of the wax: the qualities of sweetness, fragrance, coldness, and color were vividly apparent to his attentive mind. Yet a little thought showed him that his perception was not distinct; it was confused. To reach a distinct conception from a confused perception requires a process of analysis. The required kind of analysis is illustrated in his discussion, but it is not properly defined. If we are to understand it fully, we must have a more detailed picture of Descartes' theory of scientific method.

In his *Discourse on Method* (1637) Descartes laid down four rules that govern his work:

> The first was never to accept anything as true which I did not know to be manifestly so, that is, carefully to avoid precipitancy and bias, and to include nothing in my judgments except what presented itself so clearly and distinctly to my mind that I would never have occasion to doubt it.
>
> The second, to divide each difficulty I examined into as many parts as possible, and as would be required in order to resolve it better.
>
> The third, to conduct my thoughts in an orderly manner, beginning with those objects which are simplest and easiest to know, then rising little by little, as though by steps, to knowledge of the most complex, even assuming order to exist among those which have no natural order of precedence.
>
> And the last, always to make such complete enumerations and comprehensive reviews that I could be sure I had overlooked nothing.[12]

We have already discussed the first rule; it is the basis of Descartes' systematic doubt. The second rule concerns analysis; it enjoins us to divide each difficulty (or problematic conception) into as many parts or elements as possible. In Descartes' discussion of the piece of wax, we see this kind of analysis at work. The conception of wax is a complex, problematic one. As he analyzes this conception, he discovers that extension, flexibility, and malleability are the only

qualities essential to it, and as he examines these notions, he finds
that they relate to capability—of taking on an enormous number
of different shapes and sizes when flexed or hammered. The notions of extension, shape, and size are basic, however; they cannot be broken down into further notions that are simpler. Here
analysis ends.

Although extension and figure (or shape) are, by nature, simple
and distinct, they are nevertheless connected—and necessarily so:
nothing can have shape without extension—without being spread
out in space. For Descartes this fact is indubitable; we know it intuitively. If we have a clear idea of an extended object, we can
form a distinct perception of its shape and extension. But when
we do, we can see that these natures are necessarily connected;
without its particular shape, it would have a different degree of
extension, for shape is just the terminus of a thing's extension.

In *Rules for the Direction of the Mind* (about 1630) Descartes
stated that our certain knowledge is due to two basic operations of
the mind, intuition and deduction. Intuition he defines as "the
conception which an unclouded and attentive mind gives us so
readily and distinctly that we are wholly freed from doubt about
that which we understand."[13] It is clear that his knowledge that he
exists as a thinking thing is intuitive; to apprehend clearly and
distinctly that he exists is to intuit his existence. Deduction, on
the other hand, is necessarily inference from facts that are known
with certainty. Although deduction differs from intuition, it is based
upon it; for each deductive step is ideally based on intuition. To
know with certainty that *B* is a necessary consequence of *A*, one
must know, intuitively, that the premise "If *A*, then *B*" is necessarily true. As Descartes puts it:

> This evidence and certitude . . . which belongs to intuition is
> required not only in the enunciation of propositions, but also in
> discursive reasoning of whatever sort. For example, consider this
> consequence: 2 and 2 amount to the same as 3 and 1. Now we need
> to see intuitively not only that 2 and 2 make 4, and that likewise
> 3 and 1 make 4, but further that the third of the above statements
> is a necessary conclusion from these two.[14]

Intuition is thus the basis of all certain knowledge; it is needed
even for deduction. Hence, the significance of Descartes' third rule

cited above: we should start with simplest matters and then proceed step by step to those that are more complicated. Since deduction may sometimes yield long chains of reasoning, we must sometimes rely on the accuracy of our memories in affirming that a certain conclusion necessarily follows from our initial premises. We have to remember that each link in the chain was securely established by intuition. Because memory is not always accurate, error can creep into complex deductions. But this kind of error can usually be avoided by use of the fourth rule, which requires "complete enumeration and careful review."

3. Descartes' Proof of the Existence of God

Having established his own existence as a "thing that thinks" and having isolated the distinguishing marks of certain knowledge, Descartes is now ready to begin building up his philosophy. He first observes that he has already considered many things that seemed to bear what he now recognizes as the marks of certain knowledge. When he considered the simple arithmetical proposition that $2 + 2 = 4$, he certainly seemed to have a clear and distinct apprehension of its truth. Admittedly, he later found a reason to doubt this simple proposition, but his doubt was not a strong one and it did not arise when the proposition itself was considered. At the moment the proposition was clearly in mind he could not help thinking "This is certainly true." Since it unquestionably seemed to possess the marks of clarity and distinctness at that moment, may he not rely on his present criterion of certain truth and conclude that it was indeed an utter certainty?

Descartes' answer, surprisingly, is "No." Although he cannot doubt such propositions as "$2 + 2 = 4$" when he has them clearly in mind, he still finds them doubtful when he attends to the possibility that an omnipotent God or an evil genius could make him err even in matters that seem the most evident. This ground for doubt is, of course, very slight, since he has no compelling reason to believe that a deceiving God or an evil genius actually exists. But even a slight doubt cannot be ignored if he is to attain absolutely certain knowledge in philosophy. This remaining source of uncertainty must therefore be eliminated at once. This can be done only by considering whether there is a God and, if there is, whether He can be a deceiver. As Descartes admits, "until I know the answers to these two questions I do not see how I can be certain of anything."[15]

Since everything external to his mind is now in doubt, Descartes must look to his own field of consciousness for the answers he seeks. He begins by grouping his thoughts in categories with a view toward locating the special category in which truth and error are properly found. This special category is shown to consist of what he calls "judgments." A mere idea or representation, such as the idea of God or of a centaur, can neither be true nor false; truth and falsity are applicable only when something is affirmed or denied—only when a "judgment" is made. The most frequent error Descartes says he makes is to judge that certain of his ideas "resemble or correspond" to things outside him. If he merely considers his ideas as contents of his mind, they would not provide an occasion for error since he can scarcely be in doubt as to what they are.[16]

In considering the truth of judgments an important thing to investigate, Descartes tells us, is the origin of various ideas. Some ideas clearly seem to be innate, others appear to be produced by an external cause, and still others seem to have been invented by him. Thus, his ability to understand what a thing, a thought, or a truth is seems to be innate, due to nothing but his own nature as a thinking thing. But when he hears a sound, sees the sun, or feels heat, his ideas seem to result from an external cause. Finally, his ideas of sirens and hippogriffs seem to have been invented by his own mind; it seems that he has made them by putting simpler ideas together.[17] If any ideas of these three major kinds do actually represent things external to his mind, it would appear to be the second kind. Some of these ideas certainly seem to represent the things that produce them.

Descartes now proceeds to investigate this last point. Does he have adequate grounds for believing that some ideas of this second kind really do have external causes? He observes that two fundamental reasons have previously led him to adopt this belief. The first is that he seems to have been "so taught by nature." The second is that he knows by experience that some of his ideas are independent of his will, in the sense that they arise in his mind whether he wishes them or not. Thus, he sometimes feels heat even when he does not want to feel it, and he naturally assumes that the feeling is produced in him by the agency of an external thing—for instance, a hot fire near which he seems to be sitting.

Descartes criticizes these fundamental reasons in turn. When he says that he is "taught by nature" that certain of his ideas have external causes, he means that he has a "spontaneous impulse" to adopt the belief.[18] But an impulse of this kind is very different from a clear and distinct perception that the belief is true. Not only can he doubt the truth of what he believes on impulse, but he has observed that his natural impulses often mislead him when he must choose between right and wrong. A natural or spontaneous impulse is therefore a very uncertain means of distinguishing truth from falsity; it cannot possibly prove that some of his ideas have external causes.

The fact that certain of his ideas arise in his mind independently of his will is an equally uncertain means of establishing that they have external causes. It is entirely possible that he possesses an "unknown faculty" by which he is capable of producing them himself. When he is dreaming, ideas form in his mind independently of his will; yet he has no reason to suppose that those ideas are produced by an external cause. But even if he is wrong about this— even if certain of his ideas do result from things outside him—it does not follow that they resemble those things. This point was illustrated in his discussion of the wax. Although his ideas of sweetness, yellowness, hardness, and coldness may have been caused by the wax, they do not resemble the wax as his understanding conceives it—namely, as something merely extended, flexible, and malleable. The same is true of his ideas of the sun: His senses provide him with the idea of a small yellow disk, yet his understanding tells him that the sun is a sphere many times larger than the earth. Obviously, both ideas cannot resemble the sun, and his reason tells him that if either idea is produced in his mind by the sun's activity, it is most likely the one least resembling the sun.[19]

These reflections lead Descartes to the conclusion that his usual

reasons for believing in the existence of external things are inadequate to yield scientific certainty; in fact, they are due more to
blind impulse than to sound judgment.[20] He now moves on to
consider another means of determining whether some of his ideas
accurately represent something outside himself. The next means
of evaluating ideas is based on what he calls their degree of "perfection or reality." He will argue that some ideas are more perfect than others and that his idea of God is so perfect that it must
have been implanted in his mind by God Himself. His idea of
God will ultimately assure him that something external to his
mind must undoubtedly exist.

Before considering Descartes' argument, we should understand
what he means by several technical terms. In speaking of a thing's
"perfection or reality" Descartes echoes the assumption, common to both Greek Neoplatonism and medieval philosophy, that
all possible, or conceivable, things belong to an objective order
of perfection, ranging from the most perfect thing imaginable,
which is God, down to the least perfect thing, which is usually
nothingness. This cosmic order of perfection is in no sense
thought to be arbitrary or conventional; it is supposed to be
grounded in the nature of reality. The more perfect a thing is,
the more "being" or "reality" it is said to possess. God is understood as more perfect and so more "real" than an angel or a man;
and a "substance," by which Descartes means a complete, individual thing, is understood as more perfect and so more real than a
"mode or accident," by which he means an activity or characteristic of a thing. Also, as Descartes argues, if one thing is the
total cause of another's existence, the latter will owe all its
perfection or reality to this cause. In general, Descartes insists that
every total cause must possess at least as much perfection or reality
as its effect.

Descartes also relies on an important distinction between two
forms of existence, which he calls "formal" and "objective." Formal existence is simply existence as we ordinarily understand it.
To use a contemporary example, if a man owns and drives an automobile, his automobile will have formal existence; it will exist
in the full sense of the word. Objective existence, on the other
hand, might better be termed "thought-of" existence. We can ob-

viously think of nonexistent things such as Pegasus, a mythical horse with wings; and when we do, the *object* of our thought (the thing thought about) will be said to have objective existence but formal (or actual) nonexistence. Sometimes, of course, a thing may have existence of both kinds. If I think of the United States, for example, the country will have objective or thought-of existence in the sense that it *is* the *object* of my thought. But because there actually is such a country as the United States, the thing I am thinking about will have formal existence as well.

Descartes relates the distinction between formal and objective existence to his idea of perfection in the following way. All things that actually or formally exist possess a certain degree of perfection. The same is true of things possessing merely thought-of or objective existence: they too have various degrees of perfection. As a formally existing occurrence, Descartes' thought of God possesses the same degree of perfection as any other thought—the same amount, for example, as his thought of his own existence. God, however, is conceived of as an all-perfect being, whereas Descartes is admittedly limited and doubt-ridden. As the object of Descartes' thought, God therefore possesses more thought-of or objective perfection than Descartes himself. This implies, Descartes believes, that his thought of God contains more total perfection, formal *and* objective, than his thought of his own existence. Although both possess the same degree of perfection considered merely as formally existing thoughts, his thought of God can be seen to possess more total perfection when the perfection of its object also is taken into account.

With this explanation of Descartes' key ideas and terminology, we may now consider his argument. He begins as follows:

> there is another way of seeking to determine whether any of the ideas that are in me represent things that exist outside me. If these ideas are taken only as ways of thinking, I can discern no inequality among them, and they all seem to proceed from me in the same manner. If, however, we consider them as images, each representing some particular thing, then it is obvious that they may differ greatly from one another. Those which represent substances are without doubt something more, and, so to speak, contain more objective reality, that is, participate by representation in more degrees of being

or perfection, than those which represent only modes or accidents.
. . .

Now it is manifest by the natural light that there must be at least
as much reality in an efficient and total cause as in its effect. For
whence can the effect draw its reality if not from its cause? And
how could the cause impart this reality if it did not have it? From
this it follows that something cannot proceed from nothing, and
that what is more perfect, that is, contains more reality, cannot proceed from what is less perfect. And this is obviously true not only
of those effects whose reality is called actual or formal by the philosophers, but also of those ideas whose reality is considered to be only
what they call objective. For example . . . the idea of heat or of a
stone cannot be in me unless it has been placed in me by a cause
which contains at least as much reality as I conceive to be in heat
or in a stone. For although the cause transmits none of its actual
or formal reality to the idea, I must not consider the cause to be less
real. I must recognize that an idea requires for itself no formal
reality other than that which it borrows from thought, or the mind,
for it is merely a mode or manner of thinking. If, however, an idea
is to contain one objective reality rather than another, it must undoubtedly receive it from a cause whose formal reality is at least as
great as the objective reality contained in the idea. For if I suppose
that there is something in the idea which is not in its cause, then the
idea must have received that something from nothing. But however
imperfect that mode of being may be, by which a thing exists
objectively, or by representation, in the understanding through its
idea, we cannot say that it is nothing, or that the idea has come
from nothing.

Nor must I suspect that since the reality I consider in my ideas is
only objective, it need not be formally present in their causes, but
that it suffices for it to be present in them only objectively. Just as
the objective mode of being belongs to ideas by their very nature, so
the formal mode of being belongs to their causes, at least to their
first and principal causes, by the very nature of those causes. And
although it may be that one idea gives birth to another, this process
cannot be carried back in an infinite series: we must eventually
reach a first idea whose cause is, as it were, the archetype in which
all the reality or perfection that is in the idea only objectively, or by
representation, is contained formally, or actually. Thus the natural
light makes it evident to me that ideas are present in me like pic-
tures or images which, although they may certainly fall short of the

perfection of the things from which they are derived, can never contain anything greater or more perfect. . . .

The longer and more carefully I examine all these things, the more clearly and distinctly I recognize that they are true. But what am I to conclude from all this? That if the objective reality of any one of my ideas is so great that I am certain it cannot be in me either formally or eminently, and that consequently I myself cannot be its cause, it necessarily follows that I am not alone in the world, that something else also exists which is the cause of this idea. . . .[21]

By the word "God" I mean a substance that is infinite, eternal, immutable, independent, all-knowing and all-powerful, by which I and anything else that may exist have been created. All these attributes are so great and eminent that the more attentively I consider them, the less it seems possible that my idea of them could have come from myself alone. Thus, from all that has been said, it must be concluded that God necessarily exists. For although the idea of substance may be in me by the very fact that I myself am a substance, I could not have the idea of an infinite substance, since I am finite, unless it came from the infinite substance itself. . . .[22]

By reflecting on his idea of God Descartes assures himself that at least one of his ideas does represent something outside himself. His proof that God actually exists is, however, fairly complicated, and it may therefore be helpful to exhibit its basic logical structure in a more perspicuous form.

(1) I, Descartes, "a thing that thinks," have the idea of an all-perfect being, God.

(2) My idea of God actually exists; it has, as an idea, formal existence.

(3) As the object of my idea, or the thing thought about, God has at least objective or thought-of existence.

(4) Everything that actually exists has a formally or actually existing cause.

(5) Therefore, my idea of God has a formally existing cause.

(6) There must be as much perfection in a total cause as is contained, formally and objectively, in its effect.

(7) Therefore, there must be as much perfection in the cause of my idea of God as is contained, formally and objectively, in that idea.

(8) Since my idea of God is the idea of an infinite, all-perfect being, it contains objectively within it infinite perfection.

(9) I myself am an imperfect, limited being; I have doubts, lack knowledge, and the like.

(10) Therefore, by premise (7) above, I myself am not the cause of my idea of God; only something perfect and infinite could cause such an idea.

(11) Since only God is conceived as infinite and perfect, He is the only possible cause of my idea.

(12) Therefore, God actually exists, for my idea of Him must have an actual cause and He is the only possible being adequate to be its cause.

4. Concerning Truth and Error

The importance of setting out the basic structure of Descartes' proof will be emphasized below. Here we must note the consequences concerning truth and error that Descartes draws from his proof:

> And when I consider that I doubt, that is, that I am an incomplete and dependent thing, the idea of a complete and independent being, that is, of God, presents itself to me with such clarity and distinctness, . . . that I am confident that nothing more manifest or certain can be known by the human mind. Thus it already seems to me that I have found a path that will lead me from this contemplation of the true God . . . to knowledge of all other things.
>
> For I recognize, first of all, that it is impossible that He should ever deceive me, since all fraud or deceit involves a certain imperfection. Although the ability to deceive may seem to be a sign of cunning or power, the will to deceive unquestionably shows malice and weakness, and therefore cannot be present in God.
>
> Furthermore, I experience in myself a certain power of judging, which, like everything else I possess, I have undoubtedly received from God; and since He does not wish to deceive me, it is certain that this power cannot lead me into error if I use it rightly.
>
> There would be no remaining doubt of this fact if it did not seem to imply that I could never err; for if everything I have comes from God, and if He has given me no faculty for error, it would seem

that I could never be mistaken. And indeed, when I think only of God, I am aware of no cause of error or falsity; but when I turn back to myself, I recognize that I am subject to countless errors. In seeking to determine their cause, I note that there is in me not only the real and positive idea of God, that is, of a supremely perfect being, but also a negative idea, so to speak, of nothingness, or that which is infinitely far removed from all perfection. Thus I see that I am something midway between God and nothingness, between the supreme being and non-being, so that while it is true that, inasmuch as I have been created by the supreme being, there is nothing in me that can lead me into error, it is also true that, inasmuch as there is in me some element of nothingness or non-being, I am subject to countless deficiencies. . . . Hence I know with certainty that error, as such, is not something real which depends on God, but only a deficiency. In order to fall into error, therefore, I have no need of any power given to me by God for that particular purpose; I do so only because the power of distinguishing truth from falsity, which I have received from God, is not infinite in me. . . .[23]

When I consider myself more closely and examine my errors (which are the only indication that there is any imperfection in me), I find that they depend on two concurrent causes: on my power of knowing, and on my power of choosing, or my free will. . . .[24]

If I suspend judgment with regard to something which I do not apprehend clearly and distinctly enough, it is obvious that I am acting rightly and that I am not mistaken. If, however, I affirm or deny it, I am not using my free will rightly. If my assertion is false, I am obviously mistaken; but even if it should happen to be true, I am nevertheless at fault, because the natural light shows clearly that apprehension by the understanding should always precede determination of the will. It is in this misuse of free will that the privation which constitutes the form of error resides. The privation is in the operation insofar as it proceeds from me, but not in the power I have received from God, or even in the operation insofar as it depends on Him. . . .[25]

Furthermore, while it is not possible for me to avoid all error by the first means mentioned above, which depends on a clear and distinct apprehension of everything on which I must deliberate, it is at least possible for me to employ the second means, which is to remember always to withhold my judgment with regard to things whose truth is not clearly apparent to me. For although I am well aware of the weakness which prevents me from keeping the same thought always in mind, by careful and repeated meditation I can make it recur to me whenever I need it, and thus I can acquire the habit of avoiding error.[26]

Descartes is thus clear about the means to truth and the avoidance of error: assent only to things that are clearly and distinctly apprehended. To do this is, of course, to apply faithfully the method we have already discussed. By the use of this method, Descartes abandons his initial skepticism concerning the existence of other persons and an external world. Relying on the assumption that God does not deceive him—that what he clearly and distinctly apprehends must be true—he proceeds to ascertain what he takes to be the true nature of the physical world; he does this in the manner indicated above in his discussion of the piece of wax.

5. Critical Remarks on Descartes' Procedure

Descartes' point in attempting to establish the existence of God was to refute the possibility that an evil demon might confuse his mind even when he seems to be apprehending something clearly and distinctly: "may it not be that I am mistaken whenever I add 2 and 3, or count the size of the square, or make some even simpler judgment if anything simpler can be imagined?"[27] The hypothesis of the evil demon threatened the certainty of Descartes' method. If he could go wrong even in intuition, he could not be certain about anything—except his own existence. He could not be deceived about his own existence, he thought, because he must exist in order to doubt or be deceived.

It is obvious, however, that to prove God's existence Descartes had to rely on numerous premises: for example, that everything has a cause, that the reality or perfection of a cause must be as great as the reality or perfection of its effect, and so on. But surely if an evil genius might deceive him about anything other than his existence as a thinking thing, it could also deceive him about these crucial premises. Hence, it would appear that his proof of the existence of God could not be adequate to its basic purpose, which was to eliminate the hypothesis of the evil genius. If this hypothesis is taken seriously, Descartes could not legitimately trust the premises needed for his proof.

This objection was brought to Descartes' attention, and he tried to meet it by saying that God's goodness is not needed to assure us of the truth of our own intuitions when we have them, but only to assure us that when we are carrying out a chain of reasoning, we remember correctly establishing the earlier steps. But this reply is inadequate to save his proof of God's existence. As set out above, his proof has twelve steps; and if God's goodness is actually needed to assure him of the adequacy of all lengthy proofs, he could not then trust his proof unless he *already knew* that an all-powerful, nondeceiving God really existed. Hence, if he seriously assumes that God's goodness is needed to vindicate complex deductions, his proof of God's existence cannot be trusted, and his general method of deduction must then remain suspect.

It is evident, therefore, that Descartes has no real alternative to accepting the validity of his method on its own merits: he cannot possibly guarantee that it yields genuine certainty. The most he can say is that his entire method rests firmly on the idea of immediate intuition, or clear and distinct apprehension; that if a man clearly and distinctly apprehends something as true, he cannot possibly doubt that it is true; and finally that if, on this basis, a man cannot possibly doubt that something is true, he is clearly justified in assenting to it. As far as legitimate scientific procedure is concerned, he might add, there is neither point nor profit in disputing what is indubitable and obvious.*

Even a casual look at Descartes' argument for the existence of God seems sufficient, however, to question this kind of con-

---

* In replying to an objection Descartes tacitly admitted that we might, in some sense, be wrong in what we intuit, but he added that this possibility is unimportant: "What is it to us . . . [if] the truth of which we are so firmly persuaded, appears false to God or to an Angel, and hence is, absolutely speaking, false? What heed do we pay to that absolute falsity, when we by no means believe that it exists or even suspect its existence? We have assumed a conviction so strong that nothing can remove it, and this persuasion is clearly the same as perfect certitude." E. S. Haldane and G. R. T. Ross, trs., *The Philosophical Works of Descartes*, Vol. 2 (New York: Dover, 1955), p. 41.

fidence in immediate intuition. Premise (6), for example, is no doubt based on what Descartes would regard as a clear and distinct intuition; yet most contemporary philosophers would regard it as either meaningless or false. A similar question can be raised about Descartes' alleged intuition of his existence as a thinker. Bertrand Russell once objected that Descartes was entitled to claim only that thinking exists, not that a thing exists to do that thinking.

If we reflect on Descartes' proof of his existence, we can see that he did tacitly assume several principles he did not explicitly formulate. As Russell noted, he certainly assumed that thinking is an activity (or, technically, a "mode of substance") and that if it exists or occurs, it must belong to a thinking thing (or "substance"). He also assumed that doubting is a form of thinking and that if a being does some thinking, it will be fully aware of what it thinks. Since some of these assumptions have been challenged by later philosophers, it is clear that they require defense. Intuition by itself seems inadequate to justify them.

Another controversial tenet of Descartes' position is that some of our ideas are innate. In considering possible causes of his idea of God, Descartes observed that he could not form this idea himself, by "negating" his idea of finite being. Although he admitted that an infinite being may be characterized as a being that is not finite, he insisted that he could nevertheless comprehend his own finitude and imperfection only by reference to the idea of infinite perfection. As he put it: "how could I know . . . that something is lacking in me and that I am not wholly perfect, if there were not in me the idea of a being more perfect than myself, by comparison with which I recognize my deficiencies?"[28] Given Descartes' principle that there must be as much perfection in a total cause as it contained, formally and objectively, in its effect, he must in any case conclude that the only possible cause of his idea of God is God Himself.

The idea of God is not, however, the only idea Descartes regards as innate. He awards the same status to every idea he can clearly and distinctly comprehend. What are his grounds for this? In a passage discussed earlier he noted that with the exception of certain composite ideas he himself has invented, such as those of sirens and hippogriffs, the ideas he possesses are presumably either innate or else produced by his experience of external things. It is natural to suppose that most of his ideas must have been produced in the latter way, but as his discussion of the wax demonstrates, the ideas generated by experience are fragmentary and confused. His clear and distinct idea of the wax was shown to concern something extended, flexible, and malleable rather than colored, fragrant, and hard. These genuine qualities of the wax relate, as we have seen, to its capability of taking on an infinite variety of shapes and sizes—and this infinite variety is in no sense *exhibited* in experience. Since his ideas of shape, size, and motion are in this way so much richer in content than anything supplied by raw experience, he must have been created with the ability to use them in his thinking.

A further ground for his doctrine of innate ideas is drawn from the certainty and universality he attributes to intuitive knowledge. In apprehending clearly and distinctly that shape involves extension one sees, Descartes would say, that anything having shape must also have extension (or be spread out in space). But there is obviously no possibility whatever of actually experiencing everything having shape. Our intuitive knowledge therefore extends far beyond the range of our actual experience. What we know about all shaped and extended things we know *prior* to our actual experience of them; and this knowledge is possible only if our ideas of shape and extension are innate in us as thinking beings.

A final reason for the necessity of innate ideas is that we can apprehend the specific quality of our experience only if we possess ideas with which to interpret it. When Russell objected that Descartes' method of doubt did not warrant the conclusion that a thinking being existed but only that an episode of thinking occurred, Descartes might naturally have replied by asking what thinking could possibly be if it were not the activity of a thinker. Russell himself seemed to assume without question that the method of doubt is adequate to establish certain knowledge that thinking exists; yet it is far from obvious that it makes sense to speak of knowing without a knower or a knower who is not a conscious agent or thinker. Descartes, at any rate, would presumably insist that all talk of disconnected or subjectless acts of thinking and doubting made no sense to him at all. In his view you cannot possibly identify something as a thought unless you have some idea of what thinking is; and since he, like most philosophers including Russell, was fully confident that thinking (or doubting) could not occur without being known to occur, he felt completely justified in concluding that he must exist as a knower, which is a *thing* or *being* who thinks.

It was mentioned above that the assumed certainty and universality of some forms of intuitive knowledge seem to support the doctrine of innate ideas. This doctrine also seems to be supported by the assumption that mental acts like doubting cannot occur without being known to occur. If one's conception of doubting must be learned from the experience of doubting, it would evidently be possible for one to doubt *before* this learning is completed. In such a case one would doubt something without having an adequate idea of what one is doing. Yet if the knowledge that one is doubting requires, as Descartes would insist, an understanding of what doubting is, the possibility just described has the consequence that one might doubt without knowing it. If, however, this consequence is declared incredible—if it is emphatically maintained that doubting could not conceivably occur without being known to occur—then the claim that every idea must be *learned* from experience will have to be rejected.

Descartes was prepared to grant, of course, that experience has something to do with our active ability to think with certain ideas. He would even agree that infants or children greatly lacking in experience cannot actually conceive of certain things. In insisting on the innate character of clear and distinct ideas, he was rather concerned with denying that such ideas are supplied from experience, or extracted from it. For him, experience was inherently confused and required analytical interpretation. Since this interpretation cannot proceed without the use of ideas, we must already have ideas if we are to understand our experience. This does not imply, however, that experience might not activate our inborn ability to conceive of certain things; it might even be the proper stimulus for bringing certain clear and distinct ideas into play. And indeed this seems to be Descartes' view. As he saw it, experience served a necessary function in activating our ability to think. But this is very different from claiming that our clear and distinct ideas could be given by experience. The latter is impossible, he thought, because our clear and distinct ideas are far richer in content than our fragmentary experience. We can conceive of shapes we have never experienced, and we can understand what *must be* even though we are limited to experiencing what *seems to be* or what *is*.

Descartes' doctrine of innate ideas is, needless to say, very much out of favor at the present time, and it was hotly attacked by many of his contemporaries. We shall consider the most important objections to it when we discuss the rival theories of empiricism and pragmatism. Thus far, our aim has been to see the doctrine in as favorable a light as possible. We must now do the same for Descartes' theory of intuitive knowledge. This theory is just as controversial as his doctrine of innate ideas, and it is therefore important to appreciate what can be said in its defense.

The standard objection to any theory of intuitive knowledge is that intuition by itself seems incapable of settling rival claims to knowledge. What one man intuits, another man may deny; he may intuit the opposite. For example, Descartes claimed to intuit that everything had a cause; that nothing can come from nothing; that a cause must have as much reality as is contained, formally and objectively, in its effect; and that minds and bodies are distinct things (or "substances"). But other philosophers either have failed to intuit such things or have intuited something inconsistent with them. Since competing intuitions are not only possible but have been demonstrated, and since intuitions that contradict one another cannot both be true, something other than intuition seems to be needed for deciding between them. Therefore, if knowledge of certain matters is to be possible at all, something other than intuition must be found.

This objection to intuition as a source of knowledge seems very weighty, but it is not entirely conclusive. For one tning, it is not clear that conflicting intuitions are possible with respect to every claim to knowledge. Disagreement over certain matters is, at any rate, remarkably rare. Although philosophers have often quarreled about whether every event necessarily has a cause or about whether existence is a perfection, there has been little controversy about the necessity of the law of contradiction, or about the principle that if equals are added to equals the result is equal, or about the idea that a man cannot be mistaken about being in pain or believing that he is alive. The doctrine of intuition seems very plausible for these cases because they appear on reflection to be entirely obvious or self-evident, and because it is difficult to envisage anything more basic that could be used to demonstrate their truth.

These considerations gain additional force from a powerful traditional argument purporting to show that if we have any knowledge at all, we must also have intuitive knowledge. The argument begins by allowing that many claims to knowledge may be readily certified as true by an argument: they can be demonstrated to follow from true premises. The premises involved in such an argument may also, in their turn, be certified as true by another argument: they too may be inferred from more basic premises. This process of establishing the truth of a given claim or premise by inferring it from more basic premises can admittedly go on at great length. But it must stop somewhere. If we are to know that a claim is true by inference, sooner or later we must encounter premises whose truth can be known without inference. Otherwise, we could construct proofs endlessly and never know for certain that we have reached premises we are fully entitled to trust. If we do not like Descartes' word "intuition," we may characterize our fundamental premises as "directly known," as "transparently obvious," or as "such that it makes no sense to deny them." But such premises will have to exist if derivative knowledge is possible—and they will be known in just the immediate, indubitable manner distinctive of what Descartes called "intuitive" knowledge.

Descartes' emphasis on the importance of intuitive knowledge is therefore far more defensible than it might initially appear. The same is true of his theory of deductive inference, which is widely attacked by contemporary writers. As explained earlier, Descartes regarded deductive inference as based wholly on intuition. To deduce a conclusion C from a premise P one must know, Descartes thought, that P is certain and be able to see intuitively that "Since P is true, C is true" is also certain. This conception of deduction is commonly challenged on two principal grounds: first, that a valid deduction of C from P does not require that P be true; and second, that the validity of an inference cannot hinge on something as questionable as intuition.

The first of these objections is mainly verbal and is not very serious. Descartes was prepared to admit that there are forms of inference commonly called "deductive" in which the truth of the premises is not required for validity. This holds for the traditional doctrine of the syllogism. Consider the argument.

All men have green hair.
Nothing with green hair is alive.
Therefore, no men are alive.

According to the canons of valid deductive reasoning, this argument is valid even though its premises and conclusion are false. What makes it valid is that it is an instance of a valid form:

All A is B.
No B is C.
Therefore, no A is C.

This form is valid because it is impossible for it to have an instance with true premises and a false conclusion. This fact about the syllogistic form above is important because if we have an argument of that form with true premises, we shall be assured that the conclusion is true as well. Thus, in the following argument, which is also of the form above, we have true premises and, therefore, a true conclusion:

All men are mammals.
No mammals are insects.
Therefore, no men are insects.

The basic importance of syllogistic reasoning is that it provides a way of establishing the truth of what it allows us to infer from true premises. If our premises are false, the validity of the syllogism does not tell us anything about the truth of the conclusion. If we happen to know that the conclusion we reach is false, we may indeed infer that at least one of our premises is false. But if we are uncertain about both premises and conclusion, the validity of our syllogism cannot itself resolve our uncertainty.

Although Descartes was thoroughly familiar with the doctrine of the syllogism, he did not include it in his theory of method, because he regarded it as unimportant for the *discovery* of knowledge.[29] In his view the syllogism was useful primarily in systematizing the knowledge we already possess; for what is stated in the conclusion of a syllogism is already implicitly stated, he thought, in the premises and therefore could tell us nothing we do not already know. If, for example, we know that all men are mammals and that no mammal is an insect, we already know, Descartes would say, that no men are insects; we would merely articulate this knowledge if we set it out in the form of a syllogistic argument. To discover new knowledge we must therefore, in his view, employ some other method of inference. This other method is what he tried to formulate in his own theory of deduction. Since syllogistic inference is commonly considered a form of deduction, we shall avoid confusion by calling Descartes' method "Cartesian inference" or "Cartesian deduction."*

The second standard objection to Descartes' theory of deduction is that intuition provides an excessively questionable basis for valid inference. A Cartesian reply to this objection would utilize the basic argument given above in response to attacks on intuition. The reply would be based on the idea that if Cartesian inference is not a valid form of inference, then no form of inference is valid. In proof of this it would be said that whereas many forms of inference may be certified as valid by other forms of inference, some forms of inference must be self-validating or acceptable on their own merits. We have to *use* a form of inference to validate anything, even more complicated forms of inference; if no forms of inference could be taken as basic and indubitable, we could not regard any form of inference as valid. Since some forms of inference are universally accepted as valid, it must be granted that there are basic forms of inference whose validity is "intuitively apparent to an attentive mind." For Descartes, this is exactly what

---

* The adjective "Cartesian" is normally used in reference to matters connected with Descartes. This usage is derived from the form his name took in Latin writings: Renatus Cartesius.

is distinctive about such indubitable inferences as "Since I am thinking, I must exist" and "Since I now exist, my existence must have a cause."

6. Distinguishing Features of Rationalism

Descartes' approach to knowledge is a prime example of what philosophers call "epistemological rationalism." We have already observed that "epistemology" is the technical equivalent of "theory of knowledge." The term "rationalism" is also technical in this context, applying to theories of knowledge similar to that of Descartes. The term seems to have been introduced into philosophy as a contrast to "empiricism," which properly applies to the rival theory of knowledge to be discussed in Chapters II and III. As currently used, the labels "empiricist" and "rationalist" are unfortunately somewhat vague, especially since the former has become so honorific in its connotations that philosophers of most schools like to see it stamped conspicuously on all their work. Used with care, however, the labels remain useful in classifying what are essentially divergent traditions in the theory of knowledge.

Taking Descartes as representative, we may now summarize the distinctive claims of epistemological rationalism. To begin with, our knowledge of reality is at least ideally an organized structure based on a foundation of certain truth. The certainty of this basic truth is indubitable, known immediately or intuitively by attentive minds. Truth so known is of two kinds: general principles and particular matters of fact. To the former belong such certainties as "Everything has a cause" and "Thinking requires a thinker"; to the latter belong such specific intuitions as that one exists as a doubter and that one has the idea of a perfect being. All other knowledge, including that dependent on the use of our senses, is derivative from these basic certainties.

Experience, for rationalists, is inherently deceptive and must be analyzed or interpreted by the use of general principles validated intuitively. All dependent knowledge, or all knowledge inferred from basic certainties, is gained by a form of reasoning involving

Cartesian deduction. This kind of deduction does not merely articulate or make explicit what we already know; it tells us something new. Its validity is grounded in our innate ability to intuit or to apprehend clearly and distinctly that the certainty of one thing necessitates the certainty of something else.

Our knowledge of ourselves and the world is possible only because we possess general ideas by which to interpret our experience. We are capable of constructing some of our ideas ourselves, as when we form notions of imaginary beings such as centaurs. These ideas formed by us are all, however, complex; they are composed of ideas we have simply joined together. All complex ideas are capable of analysis, ultimately, into simple ones, which resist further analysis. Such simple ideas are innate; we are created with the ability to use them in our reasoning. Experience may sometimes be required to stimulate our use of some of them, but even these ideas are in no way *formed* by experience. Our general ideas always apply to more than we can possibly experience, and without them we could not even understand the experience we happen to have.

The claims just described are admittedly somewhat idealized, and not every philosopher who might be termed a rationalist need accept all of them without reservation. Nevertheless, they characterize the essential features of an important intellectual tradition, which has its adherents even today. They should be kept in mind in subsequent discussion because some of the chief contentions of empiricists and pragmatists have been consciously developed as alternatives to them—either as explicit attempts to correct their presumed error or as hopeful means of avoiding certain problems they are thought to generate.

STUDY QUESTIONS

1. What, exactly, was Descartes' method of systematic doubt? In employing this method of doubt, should one assume that every doubtful belief is false? What would be the consequences of making such an assumption?

2. How might one distinguish a rational from an irrational form of doubt? Could an utter skeptic have a rational basis for his doubts? If so, what might his basis be in a particular case?

3. Why did Descartes distrust his senses? Is his justification for this doubt acceptable?

4. Was Descartes correct in claiming that "there are no certain indications which distinguish waking from sleeping"?

5. Why did Descartes introduce the hypothesis of the evil genius?

6. What is the basis for Descartes' conclusion that the proposition "I am, I exist" is necessarily true each time he states or conceives it? What is the difference between truth and necessary truth? Why can Descartes regard himself at this point only as a "thinking thing"?

7. What does Descartes mean by clear and distinct perception?

8. What is Descartes' basis for accepting the rule that whatever he apprehends very clearly and distinctly is true? Is this basis adequate for his purpose, in your opinion?

9. What conclusions does Descartes draw from his observations regarding the piece of wax?

10. Explain Descartes' four rules as given in *Discourse on Method*.

11. Distinguish Cartesian intuition from Cartesian deduction. In what sense is intuition more basic than deduction, in Descartes' view?

12. What, according to Descartes, is the difference between a judgment and a mere idea? What is the distinguishing feature of a judgment?

13. Why did Descartes consider his former reasons for believing in the existence of external things inadequate to yield scientific certainty? What were these former reasons? What were their specific inadequacies?

14. Does Descartes' discussion in the context referred to in the previous question (13) provide a more satisfactory basis for a rational doubt regarding the testimony of his senses than his earlier argument (see question [2]) based on the premise that his senses have sometimes deceived him?

15. What is Descartes' distinction between formal and objective existence?

16. How would you criticize Descartes' argument for the existence of God? Is the argument adequate to its purpose?

17. Explain Descartes' theory of error.

18. How did Descartes attempt to answer the charge that his proof

of God's existence could not be trusted, given the hypothesis of an evil genius? Is Descartes' answer satisfactory?

19. Formulate two assumptions tacitly made by Descartes in his proof of his own existence.

20. On what grounds did Descartes accept the doctrine of innate ideas?

21. Descartes' theory of innate ideas still allowed him to credit experience with an important role in the development of human thought. What was this role?

22. Formulate the standard objection to intuition as a primitive source of knowledge.

23. What considerations can be adduced to support Descartes' conception of intuitive knowledge? On what grounds might one argue that if we have knowledge at all, we must have intuitive knowledge?

24. How does Cartesian deduction differ from syllogistic inference? Why didn't Descartes include syllogistic inference in his theory of scientific method?

25. Summarize in your own words the distinguishing characteristics of epistemological rationalism.

SUGGESTIONS FOR FURTHER READING

Descartes is one of the great writers of philosophical prose, and the interested student should make a point of reading at least *Discourse on Method* and *Meditations on First Philosophy*. There are numerous translations of these classics, but the following editions are especially recommended: *Essential Works of Descartes*, Lowell Bair, tr. (New York: Bantam Books, 1961), a very useful, inexpensive edition, written in clear, vigorous language; *Descartes' Philosophical Writings*, Norman Kemp Smith, ed. and tr. (New York: Modern Library, 1958), an excellent selection with helpful notes by an eminent Cartesian scholar; and *Philosophical Works of Descartes*, Elizabeth S. Haldane and G. R. T. Ross, trs. (New York: Dover, 1955), a paperback edition that contains the most complete collection in English of Descartes' writings.

Excellent discussions of Descartes' philosophy may be found in the following three paperbacks: Frederick Copleston, *A History of Phi-*

losophy Volume 4 (Garden City, N.Y.: Image Books, 1963), pp. 74–160; George Nakhnikian, *An Introduction to Philosophy* (New York: Random House, 1967), pp. 65–240; and Anthony Kenney, *Descartes: A Study of His Philosophy* (New York: Random House, 1968).

Two superb collections of critical articles on Descartes by contemporary philosophers may also be found in inexpensive paperback editions: Alexander Sesonske and Noel Fleming, eds., *Meta-meditations* (Belmont, Calif.: Wadsworth, 1966); and Willis Doney, ed., *Descartes: A Collection of Critical Essays* (Garden City, N.Y.: Anchor Books, 1967).

A widely used introduction to theory of knowledge that illustrates the vitality of Cartesian or rationalist principles in contemporary analytical philosophy is Roderick Chisholm, *Theory of Knowledge* (Englewood Cliffs, N.J.: Prentice-Hall, 1966). This, too, is a paperback.

Recent years have seen a revival of interest in the doctrine of innate ideas. An important symposium on this topic by Noam Chomsky, Hilary Putnam, and Nelson Goodman may be found in Robert S. Cohen and Marx W. Wartofsky, eds., *Boston Studies in the Philosophy of Science*, Vol. 3 (New York: Humanities Press, 1968), pp. 81–107.

CHAPTER **II**

Hume
and Empiricism

Although Descartes is regarded as the father of modern philosophy, David Hume (1711–1776) is admired as the most distinguished ancestor of contemporary empiricism. The basic tenets of his theory of knowledge form the groundwork of leading varieties of recent British and American philosophy, especially those that purport to be tough-minded or scientific. Hume's tools of criticism have naturally been sharpened in recent times and some of his assumptions have been drastically revised. But the root ideas of his position are still the basis of empiricism.

1. Hume's Fundamental Principles

Unlike Descartes, Hume believed that the scope and limits of human knowledge could be ascertained only by the development of a "science of man," which would exhibit the principles and operations of man's faculty of reasoning and the nature of his ideas. This science must be developed, Hume thought, by the experimental method used so successfully in physics by Sir Isaac Newton. "As the science of man is the only solid foundation for the other sciences, so," Hume declared, "the only solid foundation we can give to this science itself must be laid on experience and observation."[1] These blunt words could easily be the motto of all subsequent empiricisms.

What does experience and observation tell us, then, about the nature of man's ideas and the principles and operations of his faculty of reasoning? Let us begin with the nature of man's ideas. According to Hume, all the "perceptions" of our mind fall into two general classes: he calls them "impressions" and "ideas." Impressions comprise all our raw experiences: our feelings, emotions, volitions, and desires. Ideas, on the other hand, are the thoughts to which our impressions give rise. "Everyone will allow," says Hume, "that there is a considerable difference between the perceptions of the mind when a man feels the pain of excessive heat or the pleasure of moderate warmth, and when he afterward recalls to his memory this sensation, or anticipates it by his imagination." And again, "a man in a fit of anger is actuated in a very different manner from one who only thinks of that emotion."[2] Our immediate, raw experience differs from our thoughts chiefly in being more forceful and lively; our thoughts may mimic or copy our impressions, but "they never can reach the force and vivacity" of the originals.

This distinction between impressions and ideas is best illustrated by the difference between having a sensation and merely imagining oneself having it. Imagine, for example, that you have an intense pain in your hand. If your imagination is vivid, you might say that you can almost feel the pain. The pain you imagine is obviously less vivid than any pain you might actually feel; this, for Hume, is the basic difference between them. To think of a pain or of a sensation of scarlet is to have that pain or sensation imaginatively in mind; and to be imaginatively in mind is to be there in a faint, almost obscure way. An idea of an impression is, as he also puts it, a faint copy of an impression; the original and the copy differ mainly in their "force and liveliness."

Like Descartes, Hume distinguishes simple from complex ideas. For Hume, a complex idea is one that is built up from simple ideas by "compounding, transposing, augmenting, or diminishing" them:

When we think of a golden mountain, we only join two consistent ideas, *gold* and *mountain*, with which we were formerly acquainted. A virtuous horse we can conceive of, because from our own feeling we can conceive of virtue and we may unite this to the figure and shape of a horse, which is an animal familiar to us.[3]

Descartes would agree with Hume that we can build up complex ideas in this way, but he would disagree strongly about the origin of the simple ideas so compounded. For Descartes, the simple ideas are innate in our understanding; for Hume, they are produced by experience. A simple idea, according to Hume, is a faint replica of an original impression; and if we have never experienced a given impression, we could not possess the corresponding idea.

Hume's basis for this claim concerning simple ideas is twofold. First, he asserts that if we carefully analyze our complex thoughts or ideas, we shall always find that they are built up from simple ones, which are "copied" from feelings or sentiments we have already had. If anyone doubts this, he has only to produce an idea that cannot be analyzed into such simple ones. Hume himself has never encountered such an idea, and he is confident that no one else has either. His second argument is that whenever we question someone who lacks a certain faculty of sensation, we shall always find that he lacks the corresponding simple ideas. Thus, men blind or deaf from birth lack simple ideas of colors and sounds; if one had never experienced sensations of taste and smell, one would lack ideas of these qualities too. The last argument seems adequate to prove, Hume thinks, that a man can possess a simple idea only if he has actually experienced the impression of which it is a copy.

The principle that all complex ideas may be analyzed into simple ideas and that all simple ideas are copies of impressions is extremely important for Hume's philosophy. It formulates a clear alternative to Descartes' doctrine of innate ideas, and it establishes a useful rule by which to criticize philosophical ideas. Descartes' chief means of criticizing an idea is to declare that it is obscure or confused; but Hume thinks he can show that certain ideas are bogus. According to Hume, if we entertain "any suspicion that a philosophical term is employed without any meaning or idea (as is but too frequent), we need but inquire, *from what impression is that supposed idea derived?* And if it be impossible to assign any, this will serve to confirm our suspicion."[4]

As we shall see, this principle was developed into an extremely powerful weapon. Instead of attacking alternative philosophies as erroneous, crusading empiricists argued that the alleged alternatives were senseless.

Hume's investigation of the principles and operations of human reason was summarized in his *Enquiry Concerning Human Understanding* (1748):

> All the objects of human reason or inquiry may naturally be divided into two kinds, . . . *relations of ideas* and *matters of fact*. Of the first kind are the sciences of geometry, algebra, and arithmetic, and in short every affirmation which is either intuitively or demonstratively certain. *That the square of the hypotenuse is equal to the square of the two sides* is a proposition which expresses a relation between these two figures. *That three times five is equal to half of thirty* expresses a relation between these numbers. Propositions of this kind are discoverable by the mere operation of thought, without dependence on what is anywhere existent in the universe. . . .
>
> Matters of fact, which are the second objects of human reason, are not ascertained in the same manner; nor is our evidence of their truth, however great, of a like nature with the foregoing. The contrary of every matter of fact is still possible, because it can never imply a contradiction and is conceived by the mind with the same facility and distinctness as if ever so conformable to reality. *That the sun will not rise tomorrow* is no less intelligible a proposition, and implies no more contradiction, than the affirmation *that it will rise*. We should in vain, therefore, attempt to demonstrate its falsehood. Were it demonstratively false, it would imply a contradiction and could never be distinctly conceived by the mind. . . . All reasoning concerning matters of fact seems to be founded on the relation of *cause and effect*. By means of that relation alone can we go beyond the evidence of our memory and senses. . . . From causes which appear *similar* we expect similar effects. This is the sum of all our experimental conclusions.[5]

This passage is extremely important; it has in fact been treated as a manifesto expressing the basic commitments of modern empiricism. The crucial distinction between relations of ideas and matters of fact separates what is known as a priori knowledge from knowledge that is a posteriori. The former is said to be gained prior to experience; as Hume says, "it is discoverable by the mere operation of thought, without dependence on what is anywhere existent in the universe."[6] A posteriori knowledge, on the other hand, is gained as the result of experience; it is based on the evidence of our memory and senses. To know first-hand that grass is green we have to experience grass; we have to observe it. The mere operation of thought can never tell us what our world is like. For Hume, all knowledge of matters of fact and existence is a posteriori; a priori knowledge is limited to the relations between our ideas and can tell us nothing about the actual character of our world.

2. Hume's Conception of A Priori Knowledge

Although Hume and Descartes differ in their accounts of "matters of fact and existence," the extent to which they disagree over a priori knowledge is not entirely clear. Descartes claims a priori knowledge of certain matters of fact (such as the existence of God), but it nevertheless remains questionable whether the two men might not agree that some a priori knowledge is based on intuition. Recent followers of Hume have interpreted him as thoroughly rejecting Cartesian intuition, but Hume's words on the matter are not completely explicit. After all, he does speak of relations of ideas as being "either intuitively or demonstratively certain."

The basic issue between rationalist and empiricist interpretations of a priori truth was brought into clear focus by Immanuel Kant (1724–1804), who claimed to have been awakened from his dogmatic slumbers by reading Hume's *Enquiry*. In the introduction to his famous *Critique of Pure Reason* (1781), Kant argued that all affirmative judgments of subject-predicate form are either analytic or synthetic. An analytic judgment, when affirmative, is one in which the predicate term is implicitly contained in the subject and therefore does not add anything to the concept of that subject. Take, for example, the judgment "Black dogs are black." The subject here is "black dogs" and the predicate is "black." Clearly, the predicate does not add anything to the subject. For this reason Kant thought that such judgments are trivially true or tautologous. Negative judgments, such as "No nonblack dogs are black," may also be tautologous in this way, since the predicate may simply deny what is denied in the subject.

In *Prolegomena to Any Future Metaphysics* (1783) Kant argued that what is common to all analytic judgments is that their denials are self-contradictory.[7] Since anything self-contradictory is necessarily false, the denial (or "opposite") of a self-contradiction is necessarily true. Therefore, all analytic judgments are necessarily true, according to Kant. Their predicates add nothing to their subjects, and their certainty is guaranteed by the law of contradiction. Precisely the opposite is true of synthetic judgments. In them, the predicate does add something to what is affirmed in the subject; the denials of synthetic judgments are consistent rather than contradictory. Unlike analytic judgments, they add something to what we already know; accordingly, their truth cannot be determined merely by analysis.

Although Kant believed that some a priori judgments may be "ampliative" and therefore synthetic, modern empiricists interpret Hume as saying that all a priori truths are analytic. They deny the existence of synthetic a priori truths, and they interpret Hume as denying them as well. If they are right about Hume, it is easy to formulate his difference from Descartes on the nature of the a priori. Descartes held that the most important truths known intuitively were synthetic; this is why he did not regard syllogistic inference as a significant part of his method. If C is the valid conclusion of a syllogism with premises A and B, then the statement "If A and B, then C" will be necessarily true. But if, as Descartes thought, the conclusion of a valid syllogism tells us nothing that is not already implicit in its premises, then the hypothetical statement just mentioned will not be informative either; it will have the tautologous character of "If a dog barks, it barks."

Is it correct to interpret Hume as denying the possibility of synthetic a priori knowledge? The matter is far from clear. The chief difficulty is due to the vagueness of Hume's epithet "relations of ideas." In *Treatise of Human Nature* (1739) Hume mentions four relations "which depending solely upon ideas can be the objects of knowledge and certainty": resemblance, contrariety, degrees in quality, and proportions in quality or number.[8] If we consider that ideas of determinate colors are, for Hume, *simple* ideas, the fact that scarlet resembles vermilion would apparently be synthetic, as would the fact that red is darker than yellow. Since both these facts involve relations—namely, resemblance and degrees of quality—belonging to the list just mentioned, and since both are known merely by inspecting ideas before the mind, there is apparently little basis for insisting that they are not known a priori. If this is so, however, Hume is clearly committed to accepting at least some cases of synthetic a priori knowledge.

Commentators who have interpreted Hume as denying the possibility of a priori knowledge generally rest their case on his remark, cited above, that if a matter of fact were demonstrably false, its denial would imply a contradiction. Since the denial of something demonstrably false is demonstrably true, Hume's remark implies that anything demonstrably true must be analytic in Kant's sense. Kant's final test of an analytic truth, it will be recalled, is that its denial is contradictory; and this is exactly what Hume's remark seems to imply about truths capable of demonstration a priori.

What Hume implies about demonstrable truth is actually quite compatible with holding that some a priori truths are synthetic. Hume admits that a priori truths may be either intuitively or demonstrably certain, and there is surely no inconsistency in saying that although every demonstrable truth is analytic, some intuitive truths are synthetic. In this connection we might recall the traditional argument, mentioned in discussing Descartes, that if anything at all can be known by demonstration, something must be known intuitively and without demonstration. If Hume had been presented with this argument, he might, of course, have insisted that every intuitive truth must be empty in the sense in which "Barking dogs bark" is presumably empty. But he says nothing to commit himself to this point of view, and it might not improve his positon (as we shall see) to credit him with it.

Since the distinction between analytic and synthetic truth was not drawn by Hume, we cannot complain that he is not entirely clear about the question whether some a priori truths might be synthetic. Yet the importance of the distinction for empiricists following Hume is sufficiently great to warrant our discussing it in more detail. One question we must fully understand is why empiricists should regard the thesis that all a priori knowledge is analytic as a profound improvement over the rationalist idea that some a priori knowledge is synthetic. If we are not clear about this question, we shall not appreciate one of the major differences between rationalism and empiricism.

According to most empiricists, the distinctive feature of an analytic statement is that it cannot possibly be false. When Kant defined an affirmative analytic statement as one whose predicate is contained in its subject, he seemed to locate the source of this certainty: an analytic statement does not really tell us anything. If I say "Barking dogs bark," my remark is entirely safe—not because it shows insight into matters to which I have infallible access, but because it is totally empty. I merely repeat in the predicate what I have already said in the subject. If someone were to deny my remark by saying that some barking dogs do not bark, he would fall into the absurdity of claiming that some dogs that bark do not bark. This would be absurd and totally contradictory because what would be said in part of the sentence, "Dogs that bark," would be unsaid in the rest of the sentence, "do not bark." The total effect of such a claim is nil: each part of the claim cancels out the other, and nothing coherent is conveyed by the whole. Such claims make no sense at all; they are logically incoherent. Hence, Hume's observation that "whatever is intelligible, and can be distinctly conceived, implies no contradiction."[9]

Kant's initial definition of an analytic judgment is unfortunately not general enough to apply to judgments lacking subject-predicate form. Consider the statement "Either it will rain tomorrow or it will not." Like "Barking dogs bark," this statement seems equally empty of assertive content. But because it is not of subject-predicate form, it does not fit Kant's initial definition. His other definition given in the *Prolegomena* does, however, seem adequate to cover this case, since the statement "It is false that either it will rain tomorrow or it will not" is presumably self-contradictory. Like "Some barking dogs do not bark," the statement seems to make no sense; one cannot conceive the possibility of its neither raining nor not raining. Whatever the weather is—whatever the facts might be—the claim that it will either rain or not rain cannot fail, for it covers every possibility. Such, at least, is the empiricist's standard contention.

Descartes' view that basic a priori truths add to our knowledge in an important way is thus very different from that of the typical empiricist. For the latter, the certainty of an a priori truth lies in its emptiness: it takes no risks and hence cannot fail. Since the kind of a priori truth recognized by Descartes is not empty in this way, it necessarily takes some risks, however slight they may be. Descartes thought that we could know intuitively that certain synthetic statements could not possibly go wrong, but the empiricist typically objects that intuition is inadequate to *guarantee* such a strong claim. In his opinion if we are to guarantee a priori that a statement cannot possibly go wrong, we must have a better basis than some mysterious intuition. For him, the only adequate basis for a claim to a priori knowledge is the realization that a statement is totally empty and thus not subject to a possible risk. It is only if a statement is analytic that we may claim to know its truth a priori.

3. Hume's Conception of A Posteriori Knowledge

As we have seen, Hume maintains that our knowledge concerns either the mere relations among our ideas or matters of fact and existence. Knowledge of the former is a priori and presumably analytic; it is attained by "intuition and demonstration." But knowledge of matters of fact and existence is attained in an entirely different way; it arises wholly from experience. Therefore, a priori reasoning cannot teach us what our world is like; for this we must rely on observation, memory, and *experimental* inference.

We may assume, to begin with, that we have a reasonably clear idea of what observation and memory are. But what about experimental inference? According to Hume, all inference of this kind is founded on the relation of cause and effect:

By means of that relation alone can we go beyond the evidence of our memory and senses. If you were to ask a man why he believes any matter of fact which is absent—for instance, that his friend is in the country or in France—he would give you a reason, and this reason would be some other fact such as a letter received from him or the knowledge of his former resolutions and promises. A man finding a watch or any other machine on a desert island would conclude that there once had been men on that island. All our reasonings concerning fact are of the same nature. And here it is constantly supposed that there is a connection between the present fact and that which is inferred from it. Were there nothing to bind them together, the inference would be entirely precarious. The hearing of an articulate voice and rational discourse in the dark assures us of the presence of some person. Why?—because these are the effects of human make and fabric, and closely connected with it. If we anatomize all the other reasonings of this nature, we shall find that they are founded on the relation of cause and effect and that this relation is either near or remote, direct or collateral. Heat and light are collateral effects of fire, and one effect may justly be inferred from the other.[10]

Hume's position is clear. Observation and memory supply our basic data for reasoning about the world. We know what we observe and remember, but to know anything else about the world we must employ experimental reasoning. This kind of reasoning is based entirely on principles of cause and effect. If we know that certain foot-shaped depressions in snow are caused by human feet, then when we observe such depressions we may infer that a man has walked in the snow, whether we have seen him or not. All experimental inferences are ultimately of this type, according to Hume. We can go beyond the data of our memory and senses only by relying on principles of cause and effect.

But what is the basis of our knowledge that certain kinds of causes have specific kinds of effects? How do we know, for example, that certain kinds of dents in the snow are caused by human feet? Hume's answer is "experience":

I shall venture to affirm as a general proposition which admits of no exception that the knowledge of this relation [that is, cause and effect] is not in any instance attained by reasonings a priori, but arises entirely from experience when we find that any particular objects are constantly conjoined with each other. Let an object be presented to a man of ever so strong natural reason and abilities; if that object be entirely new to him, he will not be able, by the most accurate examination of its sensible qualities, to discover any of its causes or effects. Adam, though his national faculties be supposed at the very first entirely perfect, could not have inferred from the fluidity and transparency of water that it would suffocate him, or from the light and warmth of fire that it would consume him. No object ever discovers, by the qualities which appear to the senses, either the causes which produced it or the effects which will arise from it; nor can our reason, unassisted by experience, ever draw any inference concerning real existence and matters of fact.

This proposition, that causes and effects are discoverable not by reason but by experience, will readily be admitted with regard to such objects as we remember to have once been altogether unknown to us; since we must be conscious of the utter inability, which we then lay under, of foretelling what would arise from them. Present two smooth pieces of marble to a man who has no tincture of natural philosophy; he will never discover that they will adhere together in such a manner as to require great force to separate them in a direct line, while they make so small a resistance to a lateral pressure. Such events as bear little analogy to the common course of nature are also readily confessed to be known only by experience; nor does any man imagine that the explosion of gunpowder or the attraction of a loadstone could ever be discovered by arguments a priori. In like manner, when an effect is supposed to depend upon an intricate machinery or secret structure of parts, we make no difficulty in attributing all our knowledge of it to experience. Who will assert that he can give the ultimate reason why milk or bread is proper nourishment for a man, but not for a lion or a tiger?

But the same truth may not appear at first sight to have the same evidence with regard to events which have become familiar to us from our first appearance in the world, which bear a close analogy to the whole course of nature, and which are supposed to depend on the simple qualities of objects without any secret structure of parts. We are apt to imagine that we could discover these effects by the mere operation of our reason, without experience. We fancy that were we brought on a sudden into this world, we could at first have inferred that one billiard ball would communicate motion to another upon impulse and that we needed not to have waited for the event in order to pronounce with certainty concerning it. Such is the influence of custom, that where it is strongest it not only covers our natural ignorance but even conceals itself and seems not to take place—merely because it is found in the highest degree.

But to convince us that all the laws of nature and all the operations of bodies without exception are known only by experience, the following reflections may perhaps suffice. Were any object presented to us and were we required to pronounce concerning the effect which will result from it without consulting past observation, after what manner, I beseech you, must the mind proceed in this operation? It must invent or imagine some event which it ascribes to the object as its effect, and it is plain that this invention must be entirely arbitrary. The mind can never possibly find the effect in the supposed cause by the most accurate scrutiny and examination. For the effect is totally different from the cause and consequently can never be discovered in it. Motion in the second billiard ball is a quite distinct event from motion in the first: nor is there anything in the one to suggest the smallest hint of the other. A stone or piece of metal raised into the air and left without any support immediately falls, but to consider the matter a priori, is there anything we discover in this situation which can beget the idea of a downward rather than an upward or any other motion in the stone or metal?

And as the first imagination or invention of a particular effect in all natural operations is arbitrary where we consult not experience, so must we also esteem the supposed tie or connexion between the cause and effect which binds them together and renders it impossible that any other effect could result from the operation of that cause. When I see, for instance, a billiard ball moving in a straight line toward another—even suppose motion in the second ball should by accident be suggested to me as the result of their contact or impulse—may I not conceive that a hundred different events might as well follow from that cause? May not both these balls remain at absolute rest? May not the first ball return in a straight line, or leap off from the second in any line or direction? All these suppositions are consistent and conceivable. Why then should we give the preference to one which is no more consistent or conceivable than the rest? All our reasonings a priori will never be able to show us any foundation for this preference.

In a word, then, every effect is a distinct event from its cause. It could not, therefore, be discovered in the cause and the first invention or conception of it a priori must be entirely arbitrary.

And even after it is suggested, the conjunction of it with the cause must appear equally arbitrary, since there are always many other effects which, to reason, must seem fully as consistent and natural. In vain, therefore, should we pretend to determine any single event, or infer any cause or effect, without the assistance of observation and experience.[11]

It is thus experience, and experience alone, that teaches us the effects certain things will have and also what their causes must be. But how is this accomplished? How does experience produce the idea that *all* events of a certain kind have a special kind of cause? Hume does not give complete answers to these questions, but what he does say is extremely important. His chief claim is that the conclusions we form about specific causes and effects, though generated by experience, *cannot* be "founded on reasoning, or any process of the understanding." We form these conclusions instinctively or naturally, without any reasoning at all. And although we commonly regard the conclusions as true or even highly certain, there is no valid means of justifying them. Therefore, our confidence in their truth cannot be based on reason or understanding. It is purely instinctive.

Hume supports his astonishing view with a complicated argument in which three major stages can be distinguished.* First, he describes the kind of experience that instinctively leads us to form the belief that one kind of thing is the cause of another. Next, he explains what is involved in the idea of causation, specifically showing what must be true if one kind of thing really is the cause of another. Finally, he argues that the kind of experience

---

*Hume's presentation of this argument is very confusing, and the account in this text is designed to be simpler and more direct. Hume sometimes writes as if experimental inference always terminates in a prediction about the future, but in other passages he grants that we employ such inference to draw conclusions about the remote past as well. To emphasize the full generality of his conception of experimental inference, the author therefore relies heavily on one of Hume's accounts of causation, namely, that of an invariant conjunction between events. Hume's view of basic experimental inference is then represented as proceeding from the experience of a constant conjunction between cases of A and cases of B to the conclusion that A is *the cause* of B, where this implies that *all* cases of A, whether experienced or not, are (have been, will be) conjoined with the cases of B. Hume himself represents the inference this way in the last few pages of the *Enquiry* (see Section IV, Part II).

that generates our belief in specific causal relations is inadequate to justify the truth of such beliefs. In carrying out the latter argument Hume makes it clear that no other means of justifying the beliefs is possible and that they cannot therefore be rationally defended.

Let us begin with the first stage of Hume's argument. Exactly what kind of experience leads us instinctively to believe that one kind of thing, A, is the cause of another kind of thing, B? Hume's answer is very simple: "The experience of a constant conjunction between cases of A and cases of B." If on experiencing a case of A we have constantly experienced a case of B in close association with it, we shall naturally form the idea that A is the cause of B, and we shall expect B whenever we experience A. Suppose a man goes to a lively party and drinks his first cocktail. He begins to feel witty and gay. Not knowing anything about cocktails, he does not know why he feels happy. Perhaps it is because of the people he meets. But if he goes to enough lively parties and drinks enough cocktails, he may eventually perceive a correlation between drinking cocktails and feeling happy. If he does not have the bad experience of drinking too many cocktails, he may naturally form the idea that drinking a cocktail will *cause* him to feel happy, and he will expect to feel happy when he drinks his next cocktail. It is in this way that regularities in our experience give rise to the idea of cause-and-effect relationships.

Let us now consider the second stage of Hume's argument. What is involved in the idea that one thing is the cause of another? Hume has many things to say about this, but the following idea is crucial: If A is the cause of B, then whenever a case of A occurs, a case of B *must* also occur—and this holds for the future as well as for the past and the present. If drinking a cocktail is by itself the cause of a man's feeling happy, then whenever he drinks a cocktail he will become happy; otherwise, his happiness will be at least partly caused by something else. If someone claims that A is *the* cause of B, he can be proved wrong if a case of A occurs that is not accompanied by one of B. The claim that A causes B thus implies a prediction about the future: If a case of A occurs, a case of B *will* eventuate. A similar implication is obviously made about the past: Every A that ever occurred must have been followed by a *B*. Hume's general point, then, is that the idea of causation is the idea of an invariable relationship between events, a relationship that holds in the past and future as well as in the present.

We can now turn to the final step of Hume's argument. His aim here is to show that the experience on which our claims about causes and effects is based is not sufficient to justify their truth and that their truth cannot, in fact, be justified at all. His argument is complicated, but clear and to the point. We can justify our claims to knowledge only by observation, memory, or some valid form of inference. Our claims concerning causes and effects clearly rest on both observation and memory. We observe that certain events are now attended by others, and we remember observing such correlations in the past. Memory as well as observation is thus required for our knowledge of a *constant* conjunction between events. But claims about causes and effects do not apply merely to the present and to the remembered past; they also apply to the remote past and to the distant future. Since we cannot observe or remember the remote past and the distant future, our claims concerning causes and effects cannot therefore be justified merely by observation and memory. Some form of inference is obviously required.

We have at our disposal only two forms of inference: one is a priori or demonstrative and the other is a posteriori or experimental. The former, however, is restricted to the relations among our ideas and can tell us nothing about matters of fact and existence. Accordingly, it is incapable of supporting factual claims about the specific effects of past and future causes. Experimental inference, on the other hand, although it is the appropriate kind for reasoning about matters of fact, cannot possibly help us in the present case. When we use experimental reasoning, we always rely on principles of cause and effect, reasoning from a present fact to something inferable from it by the use of a causal principle—for instance, that a certain kind of handwriting is produced by a particular man. But the grounds for such causal principles are precisely what we are now concerned with establishing. If we were to rely on experimental reasoning to justify the soundness of our claims concerning causes and effects, we would be arguing in a circle. We would be assuming the point at issue.

Since the last part of Hume's argument is somewhat intricate, it may be useful to set it out in a more explicit form. His general aim, again, is to show that our present and past experience is incapable of supporting the conclusion that specific events have particular causes. He defends this claim by arguing, in effect, that the premise

(1) Events of kinds A and B have been constantly conjoined in our present and past experience.

does not warrant the conclusion

(2) Events of kinds A and B are related as cause and effect.

Since genuine causal relations involve the future as well as the past and present, we can infer the conclusion, (2), only if we can establish the explicitly general statement that

(3) Events of kinds A and B are conjoined in the future as well as in the past and present.

Since there is no contradiction in the supposition that future conjunctions of events will differ greatly from those experienced in the past, statement (3) cannot possibly be inferred from (1) by a priori reasoning. If the inference can be drawn at all, it must be capable of justification by experimental reasoning. But all reasoning of this kind is based on the assumption that particular events have specific causes and effects. Since the justification of such causal assumptions is what is now in question, we cannot employ experimental reasoning without assuming what we are trying to prove. Since experimental reasoning is thus not available for our purpose, and since observation, memory, and a priori reasoning are patently useless here, we must conclude that claims such as (2) cannot be rationally defended. It may be granted, of course, that we confidently make such claims on the basis of our experience and that we rely on such claims in our experimental reasoning. But Hume's point is simply that such claims cannot be shown to be true or even probable; they are not capable of any *rational* justification.

Hume put the matter this way:

All reasoning may be divided into two kinds, namely, demonstrative reasoning, or that concerning relations of ideas, and moral reasoning, or that concerning matters of fact and existence. That there are no demonstrative arguments in the case seems evident, since it implies no contradiction that the course of nature may change and that an object, seemingly like those which we have experienced, may be attended with different or contrary effects. May I not clearly and distinctly conceive that a body falling from the clouds and which in all other respects resembles snow has yet the taste of salt or feeling of fire? Is there any more intelligible proposition to affirm than that all the trees will flourish in December and January, and decay in May and June? Now whatever is intelligible and can be distinctly conceived implies no contradiction and can never be proved false by any demonstrative argument or abstract reasoning a priori.

If we be therefore engaged by arguments to put trust in past experience and make it the standard of our future judgement, these arguments must be probable only, or such as regard matters of fact and real existence according to the division above mentioned. But that there is no argument of this kind must appear if our explication of that species of reasoning be admitted as solid and satisfactory. We have said that all arguments concerning existence are founded on the relation of cause and effect, that our knowledge of that relation is derived entirely from experience, and that all our experimental conclusions proceed upon the supposition that the future will be conformable to the past. To endeavor, therefore, [to prove] . . . this last supposition by probable arguments, or arguments regarding existence, must be evidently going in a circle and taking for granted the very point in question.[12]

Hume's position on experimental inference may now be summarized. When certain kinds of events have been constantly conjoined in our experience, we instinctively form the belief that one is the cause of the other, and we then employ this belief as a premise in our experimental reasoning. Such premises cannot, however, be defended; there is no way of showing that they are true. This means that there is no way of proving that experimental inference is a valid form of reasoning. We cannot, as human beings, avoid using this form of inference, but we should realize that it is inadequate to guarantee the truth of the conclusions we reach. Our ability to reach certain truth concerning matters of fact is thus, according to Hume, severely limited; we must, of practical necessity, rely on forms of reasoning we cannot possibly justify.

4. The Traditional Problem of Induction

What Hume called "experimental inference" is merely a special case of what is now termed "inductive generalization."* As the word "generalization" suggests, this form of inference consists in generalizing from a body of data. Omitting certain qualifications, the basic rule involved may be formulated as follows: If n out of m instances of a large, arbitrarily selected class of Ks have been found on examination to possess a property P, then infer that n/m of all Ks probably have P. As an application of this rule, suppose that half of all pigs ever examined (or one out of every two) have been found to have pink eyes. The conclusion to be drawn is that half of all pigs probably have pink eyes. Again, suppose that all crows ever observed (or one out of every one) have been found to be black. The conclusion to be drawn is that all (or one out of every one) crows are probably black.

Although Hume wrote as if the conclusion of an experimental inference must always be a statement of cause and effect, his discussion of causation makes it clear that his method is just a special kind of generalization from experience. As he takes great pains to tell us, what we must establish in showing that A is the cause of B is a *constant conjunction* between events of kind A and events of kind B. Given this interpretation of general causal claims, the conclusion of an experimental inference can be formulated most perspicuously as "*All* As (or A-events) are conjoined with Bs." Since the evidence appropriate to such a conclusion is that all *experienced* As are (or have been) conjoined with Bs, Hume's method of experimental inference is nothing but a special kind of inductive generalization. To make it fit the rule given in the last paragraph, we need only take as our property P the complex property of being conjoined to a B. We can then say that since one out of every one (or all) instances of experienced

* A more specific description is "induction by simple enumeration."

As have been found to have the property of being conjoined to a *B*, probably all *A*s have this property.

Hume's argument that experimental inference is incapable of rational justification applies with equal force to the more general method of inductive generalization, and his critique is now regarded as the classical statement of the so-called problem of induction. Most subsequent philosophers have agreed with Hume. that inductive inference is indispensable for our reasoning about matters of fact and existence, and countless attempts have been made to show that such inference is justifiable. It cannot be said that any of these attempts is now universally accepted, for, as we shall see in Chapter VI, a number of important contemporary philosophers are convinced that induction is unacceptable. It is inappropriate here to survey the range of solutions that have been suggested, but it will be helpful for the understanding of Hume's position to consider the main point of one recent and influential attempt to refute him.

According to Hume, inductive or "experimental" inference is not a rational form of reasoning, because it cannot possibly be justified on rational grounds. But this claim, it is urged, is simply false. The definition of a rational being assures us that experimental reasoning is necessarily a rational form of inference. If a man were deliberating about whether to allow his children to play with a neighbor's pet lion, he would be regarded as irrational if he did not rely on inductive reasoning. In fact, if he did not consider whether in the past the lion had been gentle with children, he would no doubt be regarded as incompetent. This example shows us that it is part of the meaning of "rational" that inductive inference must be considered as a rational form of reasoning. To declare that such inference is not rational because it cannot be justified by some more basic form of inference is simply to create confusion by misusing the word "rational."'

In any case, it is unreasonable to suppose that a form of inference is rationally unjustifiable if it cannot be justified by a more basic form of inference. Obviously, we have basic forms of a priori reasoning as well as a basic form of a posteriori reasoning; if the latter were declared unjustifiable on the mere ground that it is basic, the same would have to be said for our basic forms of a priori reasoning. But this is totally absurd. To say such a thing is tantamount to saying that all forms of reasoning are unjustifiable—for we certainly cannot hold that an unjustifiable form of reasoning may justify some other form of reasoning. Since at least some form of reasoning is admitted as rational even by Hume, we may conclude that a form of reasoning cannot be regarded as unjustifiable merely because it is basic, merely because there is not a more basic form by which to justify it.

What we must recognize here is that there is more than one way in which a form of reasoning may be justified. Sometimes this may be accomplished by referring to a more basic form of reasoning, and sometimes it may be accomplished by referring to our accepted standards of rationality. A basic form of inference obviously cannot be justified in the first way, but it can be justified in the second way. This is true of inductive reasoning. Since it is our basic form of a posteriori reasoning, there is no question of justifying it by reference to some other form of reasoning. But this does not mean that we cannot justify it by reference to our standards of rationality. This justification is, in fact, easy to give. Since a man who does not follow the accepted canons of inductive reasoning in thinking about matters of fact is, *by definition*, irrational, it immediately follows that we are entitled to regard this form of reasoning as eminently rational and therefore justifiable.

The reply to Hume just sketched brings out some important points, but it does not really refute the position he is concerned with defending. Hume agrees that we do employ experimental reasoning in our everyday life; in fact, he insists that we cannot avoid using it. Although he did not state the point explicitly, he would also grant that our ordinary standards of rationality are such that the man who did not employ inductive reasoning in his deliberations about the lion would be declared irrational. But these standards, Hume would say, are merely matters of custom, and they cannot themselves guarantee that the conclusions we draw when using inductive inference are even likely to be true. The latter point is, for him, crucial; his concern is not with the fact of our customary standards but with the credentials they possess.

Hume's view on this matter emerges more clearly when we consider the charge that if inductive inference is unjustifiable merely because it cannot be justified, then any form of inference must be unjustifiable. To evaluate this charge we must first note that the general purpose of inference is, at least for empiricists, to draw true or at least probably true conclusions from true premises. If a form of inference is to be rationally justifiable, we must therefore have some assurance, Hume would say, that any conclusions it allows us to draw from true premises will be true at least more often than not. For any main-line empiricist, we have this assurance for basic forms of a priori (or deductive) inference, but we do not have it for inductive inference. And this is why we have a special problem of induction.

Take, for example, the basic rule of deductive inference, "From the premises P and Q one may infer P." We know, according to the empiricist, that this form of inference will always yield true conclusions from true premises because the corresponding hypothetical statement, "If P and Q, then P," is analytically true and empty of content. For any main-line empiricist, and we include Hume here, the same holds for all forms of deductive inference: A rule of the form "From A one may infer B" is deductively valid when and only when the corresponding conditional statement "If A, then B" is analytically true.

But now consider the rule "From the premise that all observed As have been conjoined with Bs one may infer that *all* As, whether observed or not, are conjoined with Bs."* What assurance do we have that the conclusions *this rule* allows us to draw from true premises will be true or even likely to be true? Obviously, it is not even analytically true that if all observed

---

* It might occur to the reader that the conclusion of an inductive argument should be of the form "It is probable or likely that all As are B" rather than "All As *are* B," and that this fact provides an easy means of resolving Hume's problem. Hume's response to this kind of objection is as follows. If one is to be rationally justified in claiming that it is probable or likely that all As are B, one must have good grounds for believing that at least *most* As are B. As indicated in this text, however, such a conclusion is in no way guaranteed by the premise that all *observed* As are B. We cannot, therefore, according to Hume, have any *rational* assurance that if all observed As are B, it is even probable or likely that all A's are B.

As have been conjoined with Bs, then *most* As are conjoined with Bs; the unobserved As may greatly outnumber the observed ones. Since the conditional statement corresponding to the rule is not analytic, our belief in its truth or even its high probability cannot be defended a priori. Is there any other way to defend it? Hume's answer is, of course, "No," and the line of objection considered above does not show that there is anything wrong with this answer.

As mentioned earlier, our conception of inductive inference has undergone some refinement since Hume's day. This refinement has not made the solution of his problem any easier, but it has improved our understanding of what inductive generalization (assuming that it is acceptable) accomplishes. A major lesson, emphasized in recent discussion, is that we cannot really suppose that this form of inference will ever lead us to the truth in individual cases or even to a close approximation of the truth. The most we can assume is that the method is self-correcting in the sense that its continued use will permit us to eliminate erroneous conclusions in favor of others that are, we hope, progressively more accurate. Our acceptance of the method cannot, in other words, be based on the belief that individual inductive inferences are ever likely to yield true conclusions; it can, at best, reflect our confidence that we are thereby provided with a general form of a posteriori reasoning which, if used consistently and systematically, is self-correcting and capable of bringing us increasingly closer to the truth.

To see the point of this lesson, consider the problem of estimating the relative frequency with which a certain coin turns up heads when thrown on a table. If four throws are made and heads appears only twice, we may generalize that the relative frequency of getting heads with this coin is, in general, ½. This conclusion is, however, subject to reappraisal by further inductions. If we observe a total of eight throws, three of which are heads, we shall then infer that the general frequency is ⅜. Since the evidence for the second estimate is based on a greater class of throws, we may regard it as correcting the previous one. Further throws will provide further evidence, and if we continue the process we shall hopefully move closer and closer to a correct estimate. Given certain reasonable assumptions, it can be proved mathematically that if this process were continued indefinitely, we should reach an estimate that differs from the truth by no more than an arbitrary fraction e, where e is as small as we may wish to specify.

This recent conception of induction as yielding more or less accurate estimates rather than true or probably true conclusions would not really surprise Hume, nor would he find it destructive of his basic point of view. In numerous passages of the *Enquiry*, particularly in the chapter "Of Probability," Hume acknowledged that our inductive conclusions are constantly modified by our experience of further cases, both positive and negative. Instead of discussing the relative acceptability of various estimates or the degree to which a given estimate might approximate the truth, however, he turned his attention to the purely psychological question "How is the strength of a man's belief in a certain conclusion affected by his experience of positive and negative cases?" This attention to psychological matters at the expense of a more refined theory of induction is wholly understandable, given Hume's fundamental convictions about induction. If experimental inference is not "based on reason or any operation of the understanding," he could scarcely be required to discuss how close to the truth a given estimate might be or whether one estimate is more acceptable than another.

The mathematical fact, noted above, that in the long run continued use of the inductive method would result in extremely accurate estimates cannot by itself solve Hume's problem, because the long run in question is an infinite run that can never be completed. In practice, therefore, we are always faced with the stubborn question whether our most recent estimate, made on admittedly limited evidence, is a decent approximation to the truth—and we have no a priori means of obtaining a definitive answer to this question. If our evidence is extensive and carefully assembled, we may adopt the so-called straight rule of inductive logic and conclude that our estimate is the same as what would be attained in the long run mentioned above. But we have no way of proving that our estimate is this accurate or that additional evidence will not yield an estimate that diverges significantly from our present one. Hume's fundamental critique of induction is therefore still applicable to current conceptions. Our inductive procedures are much more sophisticated, mathematically, than his were, but we still cannot prove that the conclusions or estimates we obtain are true, likely, or even close approximations to the truth.

In concluding this section we might mention that some influential philosophers accepting Hume's skeptical attitude have attempted to vindicate, as they call it, our practice of using induction while admitting that any validation of our inductive method is impossible. Their fundamental idea is that we have no alternative to using some form of a posteriori inference and that the method we do use is at least preferable to any other method we can think of. Our method is said to be preferable to others in the sense that if empirical truth is attainable by any method at all, it will be attained more readily by the method we have than by any other. Since unlike stones and carrots we are forced by nature to draw conclusions from the character of our experience, our only reasonable course is to adopt the forms of inference that are preferable to others. Since the inductive method can be shown to be preferable to all known alternatives, we are therefore completely justified in using it *even though* we cannot prove that it will bring us to the truth or to a close approximation of it.

Instead of trying to prove that the inductive method is preferable to any conceivable alternative, some philosophers have worked to establish the weaker conclusion that our accepted method is at least as good as any alternative. Whichever of these approaches is taken, however, the arguments employed are generally very technical, and they are impossible to survey in a book of this kind. We may note, however, that even these so-called pragmatic approaches to justifying induction are highly controversial. As we shall see in Chapter V, some philosophers insist that such strategies cannot possibly succeed because inductive inference, at least as commonly understood, is demonstrably untenable. The last allegation is not widely accepted—least of all by empiricists, who are virtually unanimous in accepting the inductive method as fundamental to all empirical thought. For them, as for

Hume, we might not be able to prove that induction is justifiable, but we have no real alternative to using it in our reasoning about the world.

5. *Hume and Solipsism*

We may now consider Hume's views on observation and memory, the fundamental sources, for him, of empirical knowledge. It is natural to suppose, he remarks, that our senses are capable of providing us with an accurate picture of the world around us. It is true, of course, that our senses occasionally deceive us, as when an oar half-immersed in water looks bent rather than straight. But we soon learn to disregard these deceptive appearances by further experience of the conditions that produce them. Our natural, instinctive trust in the testimony of our senses may therefore seem completely justified, but it can easily be undermined by a little critical reflection. Our belief that experience discloses a world external to our consciousness, which could exist even if all sentient beings were destroyed, turns out, in fact, to be rationally indefensible. Like our natural belief in causal regularities, it cannot be justified by the use of reason.

Hume's argument for the last claim has been extremely influential in the history of thought, and it is therefore important to have a precise understanding of its structure. He begins by observing that "nothing can ever be present to a mind but an image or perception, and that the senses are only the inlets through which these images are conveyed."[13] This observation would clearly be acceptable to Descartes: what we are *directly* aware of in perception is not the external world but rather the sensory experiences that the world presumably evokes in our consciousness. Hume reminds us of the force of this claim by remarking that

> the table which we see seems to diminish as we remove farther from it, but the real table which exists independent of us suffers no alteration: it was therefore nothing but its image which was present to the mind. These are obvious dictates of reason; and no man who reflects ever doubted that the existences which we consider when

we say *this house* and *that tree* are nothing but perceptions in the mind and fleeting copies or representations of other existences, which remain uniform and independent.[14]

When a man who is color-blind walks through a town, he will see gray shapes that he takes to be trees and houses. But real trees are not gray, and the houses around him may actually be brown. The gray shapes he apprehends are not therefore objects in the external world; they are, at best, perceptions or mental representations of such objects.

A little philosophy is thus sufficient to show us that we do not perceive the physical world directly; what we directly or immediately perceive are the sensory effects that the world presumably evokes in our consciousness. But how, Hume asks, can we *know* that our perceptions are produced by a physical world?

> By what argument can it be proved that the perceptions of the mind must be caused by external objects entirely different from them though resembling them (if that be possible) and could not arise either from the energy of mind itself or from some invisible and unknown spirit or from some other cause still more unknown to us?[15]

Descartes, we may recall, faced a similar difficulty and tried to avoid it by relying on the premise that God is not a deceiver. But for Hume this approach is totally unacceptable. The existence of God, being a "matter of fact and existence," cannot be proved a priori; and no a posteriori proof could be expected to get off the ground if even the existence of the external world were called into question.

Since the Cartesian appeal to the goodness of God cannot possibly guarantee our instinctive belief in the existence of an external world, we must seek this guarantee in experience itself. But this procedure is bound to fail as well:

> It is a question of fact whether the perceptions of the senses be produced by external objects resembling them. How shall this question be determined? By experience surely, as all other questions of a like nature. But here experience is and must be entirely silent. The mind has never anything present to it but perceptions and cannot possibly reach any experience of their connection with objects.

The supposition of such a connection is therefore without any foundation in reasoning.[16]

This outcome is no surprise. If we immediately perceive only perceptions, obviously we cannot know of the external world by perception alone. Nor can we know of it by memory, since we remember only what we have perceived or otherwise come to know by the use of our senses. Since perception and memory cannot themselves assure us of the presence of external bodies, we can know their existence, if at all, only by inference. A priori or demonstrative inference is, however, useless for this purpose, since it is restricted merely to the relations between our ideas. The only remaining form of inference is thus experimental reasoning, or inference based on principles of cause and effect. But this kind of reasoning is useless here, too. To employ it in the present case we would have to establish a cause-and-effect relationship between external things and our sense impressions. This obviously cannot be done, because to perceive a constant conjunction between impressions and external things we must perceive external things as well as impressions.

It is extremely important to understand the last point. To infer that A is the cause of B we must have experienced a constant conjunction between cases of A and cases of B. Hence, to infer that external bodies cause our sense impressions we must have experienced a constant conjunction between such bodies and our impressions. But to experience a conjunction of two things we must experience both things. Since we never directly experience external bodies, we cannot experience a correlation between those bodies and the impressions they are believed to cause. This being so, we have no rational basis for concluding that our sense impressions have *any* external cause. Therefore, our natural belief in the existence of external bodies cannot be defended. Like our instinctive belief in the regularity of nature, it is incapable of rational support.

Toward the end of the *Enquiry* Hume remarked that critical reasoning, relentlessly pursued, seems capable of destroying "all assurance and conviction." He did not, in the *Enquiry*, carry his critical reasoning to this bitter end, but it will be instructive for us to do so here. Our aim is to understand his brand of empiricism, and we cannot do this without forcing his position to its logical conclusion.

We have seen Hume argue that reason cannot justify such instinctive beliefs as that there is a cause for every event and that there is a world external to our perceptions. Is there, then, anything besides ourselves whose existence we *can* prove? Evidently not. Consider other people, for example. If we think of them in the ordinary way, as rational animals, we cannot prove their existence because they have physical bodies whose existence is just as doubtful as any other external thing. We cannot prove the existence of other minds for the same reason that we cannot prove the existence of other bodies. We never directly perceive another mind, and we cannot therefore perceive a correlation between such a mind and something we do perceive. Hence, we cannot infer the existence of other minds by an acceptable form of reasoning.

It might seem that Hume is in pretty much the position of Descartes before the latter constructed his argument for the existence of God. Concerning matters of fact and existence, Hume can apparently know nothing except that he himself exists as a "thing" that thinks, doubts, and the like. But actually he cannot claim to know this much. Has he directly perceived a *thing* that thinks? His answer is "No":

> when I enter most intimately into what I call *myself*, I always stumble on some particular perception or other, of heat or cold, light or shade, love or hatred, pain or pleasure. I never can catch *myself* at any time without perception and never can observe anything but the perception. . . . I may venture to affirm of the rest of mankind that they are nothing but a bundle or collection of different perceptions, which succeed each other with an inconceivable rapidity and are in a perpetual flux and movement. . . . The mind is a kind of theater where several perceptions successively make their appearance, pass, repass, glide away, and mingle in an infinite variety of postures and situations. There is properly no *simplicity* in it at one time nor *identity* in [all its successive] differences—whatever natural propension we may have to imagine that simplicity and identity. The comparison of the theater must not mislead us. They are the successive perceptions only, which constitute the mind; nor

have we the most distant notion of the place where these scenes are represented or of the materials of which it is composed.[17]

We have here Hume's famous "bundle theory" of the self. To the extent that he knows his bundle exists but is unable to prove that anything else—body, bundle, or God—exists as well, his position is called "solipsism." This is the view that the only thing of which a self can have genuine knowledge is that self and its perceptions, thoughts, and the like. Solipsism may seem to be about as extreme a form of philosophical skepticism as one can imagine, but there is an even more extreme form called "solipsism of the present moment." As the name implies, this form of solipsism restricts genuine knowledge to a mind's self-awareness at a given moment. It differs from the less extreme form of solipsism in regarding memory as too questionable to provide genuine knowledge. If memory cannot be trusted, genuine knowledge is consequently restricted to the present moment; for the solipsist, this means that it is restricted to his momentary self-awareness.

Can plausible grounds be given for distrusting memory? Hume says little about this, but his basic empiricist principles put memory in a very dim light. An event in the past is, in the first place, logically distinguishable from anything in the present, including a present memory event. Therefore, an a priori proof of the soundness of memory cannot be allowed by Hume. He must agree that there can be no contradiction in the idea that every memory event fails to conform to something in the past. If memory is correct on any occasion, we can prove that it is only by some a posteriori means. Direct observation is, of course, useless for the purpose, since the past is over and done with. Apart from memory, which obviously cannot be used to prove its own validity, our only remaining form of a posteriori proof is experimental inference. But if we can never directly observe the past, we never observe a single conjunction between past events and present memories. Since a knowledge of *constant* conjunctions between these events is needed if we are to employ experimental reasoning, this form of proof is also useless for validating memory. But no other form of a posteriori proof is possible.

Thus, we must conclude that the reliability of memory cannot be proved at all. This means, however, that we can have no rational basis for believing that memory is ever correct.

Hume's basic principles seem to lead us, therefore, to a solipsism of the present moment. This certainly threatens to destroy, as Hume put it, "all assurance and conviction." But a further destructive point remains to be made. Although we might not, on Hume's basic principles, be able to justify anything more than this tenuous kind of solipsism, the *idea* that other minds and an external world actually exist seems to be an entirely coherent one. The world *might*, after all, contain many things whose existence cannot be proved by critical reasoning. Hume would seem to accept this view, but it is actually ruled out by his basic principle that every genuine or coherent idea must be traced back to an original impression. If we cannot have impressions of external bodies, of other minds, or even of the past and future, we should not be able to have genuine ideas of them either. If this is so, the claim that other minds and an external world might exist, even though we cannot prove that they do, would not even make sense.

In defending his idea that every genuine idea must be capable of being traced back, ultimately, to one or more original impressions, Hume challenged anyone who might disagree to bring forth an idea that did not have such an origin. In view of what was just said, this would seem to be an easy thing to do. Consider the ideas of a thinking substance, an external world, a remote past, or a distant future. Do they not clearly refute his principle? For Hume, the answer is "No." He was well aware of such cases and tried to accommodate them by emphasizing the mind's peculiar ability to generate certain ideas from the impressions produced by its own activities. Some of these specially generated ideas are distinguished by the fact that they are not what they seem. Our idea of a necessary connection between events seems to be the idea of something in the world connecting events, but it is really quite different; it has its source in the impression produced by the mind's customary transition in imagination from the idea of one event to the idea of the event constantly conjoined with it.

Similarly, our idea of an external body is actually generated from the mind's experience of perceiving a certain "constancy and coherence" among particular classes of its impressions.

In employing this strategy to answer his critics Hume seems able to retain his theory of the origin of ideas, but he cannot avoid the conclusion that it is senseless to speak of external bodies in the usual way. When I form the hypothesis of an external world, I am not forming the hypothesis of a mere constancy and coherence among certain of my impressions. Yet, holding to his principle concerning the origin of proper ideas, Hume is committed to reply that if my idea of external existence is at all genuine or coherent, it *must* apply to features of my subjective experience. Here we can see the point of saying that a condition of requiring all genuine ideas to have a source in subjective experience is that some ideas, such as that of external existence, must be other than what they seem to be.

Apparently, Hume did not appreciate this consequence of his principle, but it has been emphasized, in effect, by his recent followers, who use it as a basic philosophical weapon. In Chapter III we shall consider some of the chief uses to which it has been put, but we might note here that its consequences can be paradoxical. Suppose, for example, that I confidently express a belief in the existence of external bodies. If my idea of an external body is, as Hume's principle requires, different from what it seems to be, then my belief *really* involves the idea that certain classes of my impressions exhibit a special "constancy and coherence." But this belief is something that Hume would never wish to question; he would accept it without reservation. If I were to insist that my belief is very different from his and concerns something I cannot directly perceive, he would have to reply that my alleged belief is incoherent and that he could make no positive sense of it at all. He could not consistently admit that my belief is, àccording to this interpretation, unfounded or false.

Because Hume's principles inevitably lead to the highly skeptical consequences we have been considering, he is often regarded as a skeptic of a very extreme sort. This opinion would be unassailable if Hume were wholly consistent and believed only what he thought he could know. But for him belief was far stronger than logic. Not only did he explicitly disavow extreme skepticism, but he frankly admitted that he was incapable of doubting the existence of all sorts of things in which men have an instinctive belief. He was a skeptic, therefore, only in believing that his many instinctive beliefs could not be rationally defended. This inability to defend them did not render them any less acceptable in his sober eyes. He was convinced, in fact, that if they were ever generally and seriously doubted, "all discourse, all action, would immediately cease, and men would remain in a total lethargy until the necessities of nature, unsatisfied, would put an end to their miserable existence."[18] For Hume, instinct and custom must be the guides in life; we must, of necessity, act on principles we cannot possibly justify. Human reason, for him, is limited, weak, and best employed as a "slave of the passions." Pursued for its own sake, it can lead only to the destruction of "all assurance and conviction."

STUDY QUESTIONS

1. What is Hume's distinction between impressions and ideas? What is Hume's basis for this distinction? Is the distinction tenable in your opinion?

2. How did Hume differ from Descartes on the nature of simple ideas? What were Hume's chief arguments for his opinion? How might Descartes have responded to these arguments?

3. What test does Hume offer to determine whether a philosophical term is "employed without any meaning or idea"?

4. What was Hume's distinction between "relations of ideas" and "matters of fact and existence"? What subjects, or studies, are specifically concerned with (1) the former and (2) the latter?

5. What is the distinction between a priori and a posteriori knowledge? Could Descartes consistently recognize this distinction?

6. What was Kant's distinction between analytic and synthetic judgments?

7. What, respectively, are the standard rationalist and empiricist attitudes to synthetic a priori knowledge?

8. Discuss the pros and cons of the question "Did Hume implicitly allow synthetic a priori knowledge?"

9. According to Hume, all reasoning concerning matters of fact is founded on a certain relation. What is this relation? Can you think of any exceptions to Hume's claim?

10. According to Hume, what is the basis of our knowledge that certain kinds of causes have certain kinds of effects? What arguments does Hume offer in support of his view?

11. Formulate in your own words Hume's argument for the claim that the conclusions we form about specific causes and effects cannot be founded on reason or on any operation of the understanding.

12. What is inductive generalization? Explain the sense in which Hume's form of experimental inference is a special case of inductive generalization.

13. State and evaluate the argument that inductive inference is, by definition, a rationally acceptable form of inference. Does this argument refute the position Hume was concerned to defend? Why?

14. Evaluate the claim that if inductive inference were unjustifiable merely because it cannot be rationally justified, then any form of inference must be unjustifiable.

15. Explain clearly the conception of induction as a self-correcting method capable of yielding progressively more accurate estimates rather than a form of reasoning capable of yielding probably true conclusions in individual cases.

16. Outline Hume's argument for the claim that our belief in a world external to our consciousness cannot be rationally defended.

17. What is Hume's "bundle theory" of the self? What are his grounds for this theory?

18. What is "solipsism of the present moment"? In what sense is this position a consequence of Hume's basic empiricist principles?

19. Discuss the question whether it would even make sense, given Hume's principles, to speak of an external world or another mind.

20. To what extent is it correct to consider Hume a philosophical skeptic?

SUGGESTIONS FOR FURTHER READING

Like Descartes, Hume was a superb writer of philosophical prose, and the interested student will find it highly rewarding to read through at least the shorter and more mature of Hume's works on epistemology, *An Enquiry Concerning Human Understanding.* Numerous editions of this are now available in paperback, but the one entitled *On Human Nature and the Understanding* (New York: Collier, 1962) is especially useful because it also contains selections from Hume's earlier and equally important *Treatise of Human Nature.*

An interesting recent commentary on Hume's *Enquiry* is Anthony Flew, *Hume's Philosophy of Belief* (London: Routledge & Kegan Paul, 1961). Hume's criticism of our idea of external existence is helpfully explored by H. H. Price in *Hume's Theory of the External World* (Oxford: Clarendon Press, 1940). The development of Hume's philosophy is thoroughly discussed by Norman Kemp Smith in *The Philosophy of David Hume* (London: Macmillan, 1941). The best short account of Hume's entire philosophy is given in Frederick Copleston, *A History of Philosophy,* Volume 5 (Garden City, N.Y.: Image Books, 1964), pp. 63–196.

Two important collections of articles on Hume by contemporary philosophers have recently appeared in inexpensive paperback editions:

Alexander Sesonske and Noel Fleming, eds., *Human Understanding: Studies in the Philosophy of David Hume* (Belmont, Calif.: Wadsworth, 1965), and V. C. Chappell, ed., *Hume: A Collection of Critical Essays* (Garden City, N.Y.: Anchor Books, 1966).

Kant's original distinction between analytic and synthetic judgments is best expressed in his *Prolegomena to Any Future Metaphysics,* Lewis White Beck, ed. (Indianapolis: Library of Liberal Arts, 1950), pp. 14–20. The acceptability of this distinction even as improved by subsequent writers is, however, a subject of current debate. Since the basic issues of this debate will be brought out in Chapter V, the reader should postpone further reading on the distinction until he has absorbed the discussion of that chapter. A list of suggested readings covering the relevant issues is provided at the end of Chapter V.

Although the subject of induction will also come up in Chapter V, the traditional problem of its justification is best discussed in connection with Hume. A very useful elementary textbook (a paperback) that discusses the standard attempts to solve the problem and also explains the basic concepts of current probability theory is Brian Skyrms, *Choice and Chance: An Introduction to Inductive Logic* (Belmont, Calif.: Dickenson, 1966). Another, rather more difficult survey of standard theories of induction and probability may be found in Arthur Pap, *An Introduction to the Philosophy of Science* (New York: Free Press, 1962), pp. 139–250. A comprehensive discussion of induction that includes an extensive bibliography is Max Black's article, "Induction," in Paul Edwards, ed., *Encyclopedia of Philosophy*, Vol. 4 (New York: Crowell-Collier, 1966), pp. 169–181. Another helpful discussion with a good annotated bibliography is given by J. J. C. Smart in *Between Science and Philosophy: An Introduction* to the *Philosophy of Science* (New York: Random House, 1968), Chap. 6.

In addition to these rather systematic expositions, useful selections from the work of important writers on induction, traditional as well as contemporary, are reprinted in the following anthologies: Ernest Nagel and Richard Brandt, eds., *Meaning and Knowledge: Systematic Readings in Epistemology* (New York: Harcourt, Brace & World, 1965), and Paul Edwards and Arthur Pap, eds., *A Modern Introduction to Philosophy*, 2nd ed. (New York: Free Press, 1965).

CHAPTER III

Contemporary Empiricism

Hume may be the undisputed founder of modern empiricism, but his recent followers have stubbornly resisted his conclusion that our natural belief in a world of trees, animals, and men rests merely on instinct and cannot be rationally defended. Convinced that genuine knowledge must be possible in such mundane matters, they have generally spurned the practical attitude Hume adopted, seeking instead some purely theoretical means of avoiding solipsism without abandoning the key tenets of empiricism. In this chapter we shall examine the most influential and ingenious of their attempts to accomplish this difficult task. Then, by way of summary, we shall offer a general description of present-day empiricism and a brief statement of the issues it seems unable to resolve.

1. *Phenomenalism*

Toward the end of the last century, empiricists began to concentrate their efforts on a very peculiar but highly ingenious means of avoiding solipsism. The position they sought to perfect has come to be known as phenomenalism. Hume had already developed the elements of such a view in A *Treatise of Human Nature*, when he tried to explain how purely subjective impressions could ultimately give rise to a firm, instinctive belief in externally existing bodies.[1] His efforts along these lines were not mentioned, however, in his later *Enquiry Concerning Human Understanding,* which he asked his readers to consider his final statement on epistemological subjects. Although John Stuart Mill developed a version of phenomenalism in the nineteenth century, it was not until the present century was well under way that the position received its clearest, most explicit formulation and defense. Like ideals of other kinds, it came to full flower (but then died) in the period between the two world wars.

The fundamental tenet of phenomenalism was well expressed by Mill when he said that physical things are merely "permanent possibilities of sensation."[2] Instead of regarding trees and houses as independent objects knowable, if at all, only by their effects on our consciousness, phenomenalists treat them as a kind of construct out of sensory experiences. To appreciate this approach consider a large red ball. What would we normally mean in saying that such a thing exists? When we say that it is red presumably we mean that a normal observer would experience redness if he looked at it; and when we say that it is round evidently we mean that an observer would see something round if he looked at it or feel something round if he felt it. Apparently, in both instances we mean that observers *would have certain experiences* in its presence. Of course, there is far more to a red ball than the specific experiences it happens to give existing observers. We must also consider the range of experiences it would give all possible observers *if* they perceived it under a variety of conditions. A red ball is the sort of thing, for example, that would look black to any normal observer viewing it in a very dark room.

According to the phenomenalist, the import of what we mean in speaking of so-called physical objects is exhausted by facts about human experiences. If I say that there is a large yellow dog in the next room, then if you were to have the experiences of being in that room and of having your eyes open, you would have the experience of seeing such a dog. What we mean in speaking of a yellow dog does not, at least in everyday life, have anything to do with something imperceptible, which may merely cause us to have certain experiences. Admittedly, we do believe that dogs, like most mobile things, are likely to interact causally with other things; they are apt, for example, to knock over lamps. Yet, as we know from Hume, all we can reasonably mean by a causal inter-action is that certain events are conjoined and that they are in-stances of kinds of events that are always so conjoined. To say that a dog knocks over a lamp is only to imply, therefore, that suitably placed observers will have experiences of a dog jumping followed by experiences of a lamp falling and that other observers would also have such experiences if they too were suitably placed.

An interpretation of this kind may appear plausible for balls, lamps, and perhaps even dogs, but what about observers and their various positions in the world? Can they possibly be under-stood in a similar way? The phenomenalist's answer is "Yes." As Hume also taught us, if we attend carefully to the nature of our own selves, we shall find nothing but a complex bundle of experi-ences. We undoubtedly think of ourselves as much more than a bundle: we think of ourselves as unitary agents that may live for some time relatively unchanged. But this conception of our selves is as uncritical as it is untenable, and we naturally have it only because the bundles we actually are hang together in a way that creates an illusion of unity and permanence. As far as actual facts rather than natural beliefs are concerned, we have no real alternative to the strict view of Hume that even selves or observ-ers are complex systems of experiences.

As for our position in the world, how could we possibly make sense of something so abstract, if not in terms of distinctive ex-periences? I am now in my study, awake and alert. What this im-plies is that my current thoughts occur against the background of a familiar class of experiences and that anyone truly described as "in the study with me" will also have such experiences. From my point of view, these background experiences are distinctive in two ways: they are directly associated with the words "my study," and they are closely related to further experiences associated with such words as "my house" and "this earth." These related experi-ences are very important to my idea of my study, for they make it the idea of *a certain place on earth*. Someone else's study could conceivably be an exact replica of mine in respect to the experi-ences it directly involves, but the difference between the two places stands out clearly when their related experiences are taken into account. The idea of my study as a unique location, as one special place in a network of many places, is therefore somewhat complicated. But it still involves nothing but concrete facts of human experience.

In view of the claims just made it might seem that if the phenomenalist is right, the world of people, houses, lamps, and dogs must be a kind of collective hallucination. The phenomenalist may allow that there is a germ of truth in this idea, but certainly no more than that. As he sees it, there is an obvious difference between hallucinations and real things, and this difference is best described in terms of his theory. Consider, for example, the hallucinatory dagger experienced by Macbeth. To determine that this dagger was not a real one it was not necessary for Macbeth to disprove the existence of a certain external cause of his dagger experiences. All he had to do was observe that certain experiences invariably associated with real daggers were strangely missing. He tried to clutch the dagger, but it appeared to pass through his fingers, giving him no sensations of touch. If these missing sensations distinctive of daggers had actually been present and available to other observers, a real dagger would unquestionably have existed. In the case of any hallucination, whether private or collective, certain necessary elements of human experience are conspicuously absent; and it is this, rather than the absence of an alleged external cause, that distinguishes them from the real thing.

The position of the phenomenalist is not merely, as the preceding discussion might imply, that everything we can possibly *know* about external things is limited to facts about human experience. It is also that everything we can legitimately *mean* in speaking of these things must be limited to such facts. The latter claim is a consequence of Hume's principle that all genuine or legitimate ideas must be capable of being traced back to original impressions. Since it is impossible to have an impression of an unexperienced external cause, a genuine idea of such a thing cannot possibly be formed. If our common ideas of external things are to be regarded as legitimate, we must therefore agree that they arise solely from original ideas derived from sensory experiences. A philosophically useful way of expressing this is to say that any so-called external thing we can genuinely conceive of must be understood as a mere "construct" out of sensory experiences.

The kind of phenomenalism just described underwent considerable refinement and qualification during the early decades of this century and became an exceedingly subtle and sophisticated position. In spite of all this refinement, however, the position remained inherently untenable, at least when viewed as an alternative to solipsism. The inevitable failure of this view was due to its interpretation of a physical thing in relation to the experiences of all sorts of observers under all sorts of conditions. Although such generality was needed to give the position an air of plausibility, it is unfortunately incompatible with the knowledge a phenomenalist can be expected to possess. How is he to know, after all, what sort of experiences other observers would have under all sorts of conditions? In fact, what could he possibly know about *any* experience belonging to some other person? The only answer permitted the phenomenalist by his strict empiricist assumptions is "Nothing at all." And this answer thoroughly undermines his position.

In this connection ·we must remember that the fundamental aim of the phenomenalist was to avoid Hume's skeptical conclusions regarding the existence of a public world of trees, animals, and men. As long as this world was admitted to be something strictly external to our consciousness, its existence seemed rationally unfounded, given Hume's empiricist principles. To avoid this consequence and to establish a rational basis for the mundane beliefs of common life the phenomenalist argued that the natural world is not really something external to our consciousness but merely a construct fabricated from our sensory experiences. Although this approach seemed adequate to by-pass Hume's skeptical line of argument without abandoning the basic tenets of empiricism, it actually required a fund of knowledge about other minds that is every bit as questionable on Hume's empiricist principles as the supposed knowledge of a genuinely external world.

As we saw in discussing Hume's philosophy, the skeptical consequences of his fundamental principles extend to everything external to his consciousness, not just to the alleged external causes of his perceptions. This holds true even if memory and induction are granted to be valid sources of knowledge. Since the phenomenalist, in seeking a means of avoiding Hume's skeptical conclusions regarding external objects, implicitly accepted Hume's basic epistemic principles, he cannot consistently claim the knowledge of other minds required to make his theory of the natural world succeed. To by-pass the full extent of Hume's skeptical conclusions, the phenomenalist would have had to avoid all reference to things he cannot directly perceive. But had he done this, his alternative to Hume would not even have appeared to get off the ground.

The last point is extremely important, because any form of phenomenalism attempting to construe physical things as constructs out of the experience of a single mind or observer would be, at best, a weakly disguised form of solipsism. A single observer may construct an organized picture of reality from his experience, but he cannot seriously maintain that the picture he constructs is in any way identical with the public reality we all believe to exist. There is, after all, a crucial difference between that reality and the appearances it presents to individual observers. Each of us views the world from a limited perspective and possesses equally limited powers of discrimination. Some of us are deaf, some of us are blind, and most of us are insensitive to the wide range of smells and tastes so important to perfumers and wine-tasters. The suggestion that the whole of reality might be identified with the special view that any one of us could generate, even in the longest of long runs, is simply absurd. The "objects" that could be constructed from the experiences of a single consciousness would be the objects of a solipsist's world; they would certainly not be identical with that public reality in which we instinctly believe.

Despite all the attention it has received, the promise of phenomenalism turns out therefore to be illusory. If it does not require more knowledge than the traditional empiricist can possibly justify, it cannot get him beyond solipsism. The failure of after the end of World War II its failure was acknowledged by phenomenalism was not seen in the terms presented here, but most empiricists. This outcome brought some philosophers back to the position of Hume: they insisted that solipsism is as irrefutable as it is unbelievable and that our only alternative is to follow our instincts and accept the natural or naïve view of things, which we cannot rationally defend. Other philosophers continued to find this practical solution unacceptable, arguing instead that Hume's fundamental epistemic assumptions require thorough reevaluation. The source of all his skeptical difficulties seems to be his assumption that we directly experience our impressions rather than external things. But this assumption does not have to be accepted without question. Its repudiation has, in fact, been the starting point of present-day empiricism.

2. *The Proper Objects of Perception*

When Hume introduced his idea that our senses are, at best, inlets through which perceptions are conveyed to our mind, he illustrated his meaning by remarking that as we move away from a table it seems to diminish in size. Since presumably the table does not change in this way, the conclusion to be drawn is that we must be seeing a series of mental images that represent the table to us. This inference is far from convincing, however. There is nothing in the facts described that requires us to introduce any object of perception other than the table. We may simply say that we continue to see the table but that it seems to *look* smaller as we move away from it. By describing the facts in this way, we do not introduce a logical gap between the table and ourselves, which we would be required to bridge by some dubious form of inference.

There are times, of course, when this simple form of description is inadequate. If, for example, we have a hallucination or a dream that we are being attacked by a bear, we cannot say that we are seeing something real, which merely looks different from the way it is. Yet even in these cases it is not necessary to say that we are seeing a special mental object. Instead, we might say that although we seem to see something strange or frightening, we do not actually see anything at all, since nothing is there.

To this we may add that the inference from "I thought or imagined or dreamed that something was there" to "I perceived something" is simply invalid. Thinking, imagining, and dreaming are not to be counted as forms of perception. When we have genuine perception, we must admit a perceived object. But we can, as in hallucinations or dreams, believe we are perceiving something when we are not; in these cases it is not necessary to introduce a special object of our awareness.

It may be objected that Hume's problems cannot possibly be avoided by this strategy because there are, as Descartes noted, "no certain marks" by which dreaming or even hallucinating can be distinguished from waking experience. This holds even if genuine perception differs from dreams and hallucinations in requiring a perceived object; for the question can always arise whether we are—or merely think, dream, or imagine that we are—apprehending a genuine object. If we cannot tell by our experience whether we are apprehending a genuine object, then Hume's skeptical conclusions still hold good, even if they must be formulated differently. Therefore, to deny that hallucinations and dreams require special objects of perception does not help us avoid the problem of solipsism; it merely requires that we formulate the problem in slightly different terms.

Recent empiricists commonly attack this kind of reply on two chief grounds. First, they argue that we do understand the difference between dreaming, hallucinating, and having genuine perceptions, and that this understanding would not be possible if we did not have criteria by which to distinguish genuine perception from these other, more delusive states of mind. If we can really understand the question "Am I dreaming or awake? or am I hallucinating?" then we must know how to answer it; otherwise, they insist, the distinction between perceiving, dreaming, and hallucinating would not make sense to us.

Their second line of argument is a development of the first. It is not merely, they argue, that we can *in principle* distinguish dreaming and hallucinating from genuine perception, but that we make these distinctions every day of the week and do so with great confidence. If, for example, I am not actually seeing but merely hallucinating a floating dagger, I will not be able to catch hold of it no matter how hard I try. If I were able to hold on to it and use it to stab someone, the dagger would obviously be real rather than hallucinatory. As far as dreams are concerned, it is simply false that they are indistinguishable from waking experience. Dreams obviously have a distinctive quality that is not present in waking experience, and the relief felt in awakening from a bad dream is unmistakable. The claim, therefore, that we have no way of telling whether we are dreaming, hallucinating, or actually perceiving something is unfounded in fact, and it cannot possibly support philosophical skepticism.

It is important to realize that when we do dream or hallucinate, we interpret our experience with the aid of concepts strictly applicable to public things. If I dream that I am seeing a bear or hallucinate the presence of one, in either case I am using my concept of a bear to interpret my experience. The same is true of all cases in which we may *seem* to be seeing something: what we seem to see is always some objective entity—a bear, a rat, an oasis in the distance. When, similarly, we wish to describe our impressions and ideas, we inevitably allude to some kind of physical thing. Hume himself spoke of house or tree perceptions, and we all identify images and ideas by reference to the public objects they represent. The fact that we commonly describe our subjective states in this way is extremely important, and recent empiricists have argued that it discloses a fatal error in Hume's account of perception.

Hume's skeptical argument makes it clear that the idea of a mind-independent, public object cannot be derived from subjective impressions. But the remarks made above suggest that our ideas of subjective impressions are built up from our ideas of public things. This seems to indicate that our ideas of public things are more basic than our ideas of subjective impressions and that our knowledge of public things is more basic than our knowledge of our own impressions. To understand the description "the experience of seeing a red ball" we must know what a red ball is— and a red ball is a public object. If, as the last paragraph suggests, we always describe our subjective experiences in relation to public

objects, the knowledge that such descriptions are appropriate
would imply a large body of knowledge about the character of the
external world.

One may reply, of course, that although we do commonly conceive of our subjective experience in relation to external objects,
we *can* conceive of them without such a reference. This kind of
reply has been countered, however, by a highly influential argument of Ludwig Wittgenstein's. His argument is far too cryptic
and complicated to be cited here, but its basic import has been
clearly expressed by Norman Malcolm, a philosopher sympathetic to Wittgenstein's point of view:

> one supposes that one inwardly picks out something as thinking or
> pain and thereafter identifies it whenever it presents itself in the
> soul. But the question to be pressed is, Does one make *correct*
> identifications? The proponent of these "private" identifications has
> nothing to say here. He feels sure that he identifies correctly the
> occurrences in his soul; but feeling sure is no guarantee of being
> right. Indeed, he has no idea of what being *right* could mean. He
> does not know how to distinguish between actually making correct
> identifications and being under the impression that he does. . . .
> Suppose that he identified the emotion of anxiety as the sensation
> of pain? Neither he nor anyone else could know about this "mis-
> take." Perhaps he makes a mistake *every* time! Perhaps all of us
> do! We ought to know now that we are talking nonsense. We do
> not know what a *mistake* would be. We have no standard, no
> examples, no customary practice, with which to compare our inner
> recognitions. The inward recognition cannot hit the bull's eye, or
> miss it either, because there is no bull's eye.*

What is being challenged here is the assumption, accepted as
obvious by Descartes and Hume, that a man cannot possibly
be wrong about the character of his subjective experiences.
Since a subjective experience is distinguishable from the *belief*
that one has a certain kind of experience, it would appear that the
belief could occur without the experience and that the experience
could occur without the belief. If this is possible, the belief can-

---

* Norman Malcolm, *Knowledge and Certainty: Essays and Lectures* ©
1963, p. 138. Reprinted by permission of Prentice-Hall, Inc., Englewood
Cliffs, New Jersey.

not guarantee its own truth; an independent guarantee is required. But what, in subjective experience, could provide such a guarantee? Wittgenstein's answer is "Nothing." It might seem that memory could provide such a guarantee: "The thing I am now experiencing must be a pain because I can remember calling similar things 'pains' in the past." But Wittgenstein rejects this possibility, arguing that subjective experience is by itself inadequate to justify the reliability of memory. We may seem to remember having called certain things "pains" in the past, but we cannot have a subjective guarantee that memory impressions are ever correct. To have any genuine knowledge, we must be able to appeal to something *independent* of our subjective impressions—and this holds for memory as much as for anything else.

Wittgenstein's claim is not merely that subjective experience is by itself inadequate to justify claims to knowledge; he also maintains that we could not make sense of the word "knowledge" or the word "pain" on a purely subjective basis. He argues that we can make sense of a descriptive expression only if we are capable of establishing conclusively that it is correctly or incorrectly used. Since subjective experience cannot itself assure us that our use of the words "knowledge" and "pain" is actually correct, it follows that we cannot make sense of these words on a purely subjective basis.

Our everyday use of words does not face these limitations because we are clearly capable of appealing to something independent of our mere impression that we use them correctly—namely, the testimony of other people. This testimony is of crucial importance because as children we were taught to use language by our parents and teachers, and it was their job to make sure that we learned it correctly. The word "red," for example, has a conventional meaning; it applies *by convention* to a particular color. We were taught as children to use the word in reference to this color, and when we made mistakes we were promptly corrected. The same is true of such words as "pain": they too are learned in a social context. It is under the guidance of our fellows that we learn to associate "pain" or "itch" with certain feelings, and by the time we are adults this association is so firmly established that we rarely make a mistake when applying the words to ourselves. The habit of using these words is drilled into us as a matter of social training, and the standards governing their correct use are social as well. All this underlines the importance of being able to check our claims by an appeal to the testimony of others.

For Wittgenstein, social norms and community agreement in the proper use of language are the touchstones of empirical truth. We learn to speak in a social context, and the success of our verbal efforts is determined by social standards. Since so-called external objects are the ones conspicuously available for community reference, it is these objects rather than subjective experiences that constitute the subject of our most secure empirical knowledge. Earlier empiricists insisted that such knowledge must be highly uncertain, but their arguments were rooted in a false analysis of what knowledge is. They believed that the highest grade of knowledge is wholly subjective and that all other knowledge must be inferred from what is peculiar to each man's solitary consciousness. But this belief puts the cart far before the horse. Empirical knowledge is a community phenomenon, and it is necessarily based on data available to all.

3. *The New Empiricism and Its Problems*

Although the extent to which Wittgenstein was an empiricist is somewhat unclear, recent defenders of Wittgenstein generally fall squarely in the tradition of Hume. Like Hume, they tend to accept the thesis that all a priori knowledge is analytic, and they usually accept his root assumptions concerning matters of fact and existence. Of course, they reject his idea that observational knowledge strictly concerns each man's subjective experience; for them, such knowledge concerns public objects. But aside from this reservation, the new empiricists follow Hume's key principles very closely. They regard observation and memory as the basic sources of empirical knowledge; they argue that all acceptable reasoning concerning matters of fact and existence is based on inductive generalization; and they insist that all meaningful concepts must ultimately relate to experience. This similarity between the new empiricism and Hume's empiricism is extremely important, because the new empiricism faces problems that are closely related to the ones that troubled Hume.

One problem for the new empiricist concerns the justification of induction. On strict empiricist principles this problem remains alive because even though we may commonly accept induction as a rational form of inference and regard those who do not employ it properly as ignorant, irrational, or illogical, we cannot prove that the conclusions we obtain by its use are true, true more often than not, or even close approximations of the truth. This fundamental difficulty was discussed in Chapter II, where the limitations of a defense based on the fact of our existing conventions were mentioned. Pragmatists, who build their philosophy on the premise that all empirical knowledge is essentially uncertain and that absolutely secure knowledge is a visionary ideal, can perhaps take this difficulty about induction in their stride. But it remains an important source of concern for reflective empiricists unwilling to accept the consequences of a thoroughgoing pragmatism.

On the assumption, however, that induction, memory, and ordinary observation are acceptable sources of knowledge, the new empiricist has no trouble avoiding Hume's problem about the external world. He can also avoid Hume's specific problems about minds, both one's own and those of others. Since we have already described the new empiricists's defense of our perceptual knowledge of a public "external" world, we shall now consider what he has to say about minds. His views on this subject will disclose the strength as well as the weakness of his general position.

Hume's problem concerning his own mind arose because his introspection failed to disclose a self distinct from swarms of impressions and ideas. Since the new empiricist does not attempt to extract his basic knowledge from introspection, Hume's failure to introspect a distinct self is, for him, philosophically unimportant. As he sees it, the concept of a self or person must be intersubjective, and the thing to which it applies must be publicly recognizable. This fact accords with ordinary beliefs. Only a philosopher would suppose that selves might be other than the living beings we can see, touch, and talk to. Once Hume's subjective basis for factual knowledge is abandoned, this natural belief can be accepted without reservation. A self is then seen to be a living being of flesh and blood who is a conspicuous member of a visible community. Hume's failure to introspect his self is, from this natural point of view, just what one should expect. To gain a full view of one's self, it would be wise to look in a mirror; for a self is a human being—not an immaterial spirit or a peculiar bodiless aggregate of feelings and thoughts.

Although this common-sense belief regarding selves is difficult to dispute, it might appear that a man's *mind*, at any rate, is an immaterial object not available for intersubjective scrutiny. This suggestion is unacceptable to the new empiricist, however. For him, a man's mind is not an object at all—and it cannot, therefore, be an immaterial one. To show that a man has a mind, it is sufficient to establish that *he* is capable of thinking, feeling, and acting intentionally. This is easily done by asking him questions, pricking him with pins, and the like. If he can answer the questions, solve simple problems, and react to sensory stimulation, there can be no question of his not having a mind. To have a mind is, we might say, to be *capable* of thinking, feeling, and acting with purpose. It is this capability that is crucial, since a man still has a mind when he is so deeply asleep that he is not even dreaming. For him literally to lose his mind he must stop being a man and become a corpse. To have a mind is not, therefore, to be possessed of a peculiar Cartesian object; rather, it is to have the mental *capacities* and *abilities* distinctive of a living human being.

This conception of minds and selves seems to resolve both Hume's problems about minds. It shows each man what his own mind is, and it justifies his beliefs about the minds of others. If to have a mind is to be capable of thinking, feeling, and acting intelligently, then we can easily establish the existence of other minds by putting questions to people, setting simple problems for them to solve, stimulating them with pins and feathers, and then observing their responses. If they give intelligent answers to our questions, solve the problems we set them, and laugh or cry when we stimulate them, they will conclusively demonstrate that they are intelligent, sentient creatures. Any philosophical doubts about whether people who behave in this way really have minds will not make sense, for the meaning we attach to the word "mind" guarantees that it applies to such people.

There is so much merit in this approach to Hume's problems regarding minds that it is difficult to find any flaw in it. A problem emerges, however, if instead of asking how we know other people have minds, we ask how we can know that they have feelings such as pain. Wittgenstein's answer, that we can observe their pain behavior (their tears, cries, and jerky movements), does not seem entirely satisfactory, since we normally regard a feeling as something very different from such behavior. If this normal supposition is correct, we are apparently justified in asking how mere observable behavior can possibly guarantee the presence of a feeling, which is not open to view. Is it not possible, we may ask, for a man to exhibit pain behavior and yet not be feeling pain? This certainly does seem possible, and it prompts the question "How can we possibly know, merely from observing his behavior, whether he has a certain feeling?" This question is not answered by the considerations mentioned in the last paragraph, because we can evidently raise the question even when we are assured that the man we are talking about *is* an intelligent agent and does react to our pins and needles.

The problem here is really part of the old problem that bothered Hume. If feelings and even certain thoughts are subjective states distinguishable from the behavior people can be observed to display, then any generalization relating such thoughts and feelings to external behavior must be synthetic and knowable only by experimental reasoning. Such reasoning is useless in this case, however, since we can never observe another man's feelings and thus establish a constant conjunction between his feelings and certain forms of his behavior. Assuming that we can observe our own behavior (rather than our subjective impressions of it), we may be able to discover a constant conjunction between it and certain feelings that we have, but this will not establish a general relation suitable for inferences concerning the feelings of anyone else. The latter is impossible on Hume's principles because if we were to generalize from our total data concering feelings and behavior, we would have to conclude that by far the greatest proportion of all behavior is probably not accompanied by feelings. This conclusion would be inevitable because each of us is constantly surrounded by a crowd of friends or neighbors whose inner feelings are not apparent to us when they openly smile, sigh, or sob.

One way of mitigating this difficulty, adopted by Mill and Russell, is to avoid inductive generalization in favor of an argument by analogy. The latter kind of argument may be founded on the principle that similar effects probably have similar causes, whether those causes are observable or not. Given that we may easily establish that certain of our own experiences have distinctive behavioral effects, the principle allows us to infer that similar behavior on the part of other persons is probably brought about by causes similar to those experiences. Assuming that nothing can be similar to an experience but another experience, we may then conclude that other people probably have experiences too.

Anyone employing this kind of argument must, of course, offer good reason for accepting the principle of analogy and also for preferring the conclusion it yields to the one strictly required by Hume's method of induction. Since the two conclusions are based on the same total data and yet are logically inconsistent, a philosopher can regard one as more probable than the other only if he can show that the reasoning behind it has greater merit and authority. A crucial question he should answer if he prefers the conclusion from analogy is whether the principle involved is in general more weighty than ordinary induction or whether there is something special about the case of other persons' experiences that renders the use of Hume's method inappropriate.

Any orthodox empiricist is certainly not likely to grant that inductive inference is, in general, less weighty than some other form of a posteriori inference. He will say that if we are right to prefer the conclusion of the analogical argument, it can only be due to some special feature of the present case that renders induction inapplicable. Such a feature seems, in fact, easy to identify: it is the radical subjectivity of human experience. As a matter of definition, an individual person's experience is directly apparent only to himself. In consequence of this, we could not hope to know of another's experience by direct observation. Our failure to observe a correlation between the experience and behavior of others is therefore just what we should expect, and it clearly should not support the conclusion that others probably have no experiences. To deny that this conclusion is supported by what we observe, or fail to observe, is not to reject the validity of inductive generalization; it is merely to acknowledge that its application is properly restricted to things we can expect to observe. For things of other kinds—for things *unobservable in principle*—inductive generalization is simply inapplicable.

Assuming that we may thus avoid drawing the conclusion Hume's method strictly requires, what can we say in defense of the principle of analogy? One standard answer is that arguments based on this principle have essentially the same status as those involving inductive generalization. Neither form of argument can be validated in the sense of being shown to yield true or even approximately true conclusions from true premises at least more often than not. But we do use them about equally often in science and everyday life, and we seem to place equal confidence in the conclusions they allow us to reach. Our belief, for example, that those we know and love best—our children, spouses, parents, friends—have all kinds of feelings and all kinds of thoughts is vastly stronger than the vague belief that the future will, as Hume puts it, "be conformable to the past." And if the inductive reasoning based on the latter belief is in any degree justifiable, it is equally justifiable to reason in accordance with the principle of analogy.

Although a tempting case can undoubtedly be made for the acceptability of analogical reasoning, such reasoning may nevertheless yield conclusions running counter to fundamental empiricist commitments. This holds true of the conclusion concerning experiences that are unobservable in principle: any strict empiricist is bound to reject it at once. The philosophers we have called the new empiricists are especially strict in this regard; they insist that analogical reasoning is illegitimate whenever it exceeds the limits of the observable. To be fully acceptable in their view, an instance of analogical reasoning must, in fact, be capable of validation by ordinary induction. The latter is, for them, our fundamental form of a posteriori reasoning, and any acceptable non-deductive argument must in some way be based upon it.

As compared with inductive generalization, the peculiarity of the form of analogical inference allowed by empiricists is that it directly yields specific rather than general conclusions: it affirms that *certain things* probably have some property because they are similar to things that are known to have that property. Since the similarity of two things consists in their possession of common features or properties, the force of an analogical argument can be represented by saying that certain things with, say, the properties A, B, and C will probably also have the property D because all examined or known things with A, B, and C have D.* As we have seen, however, the premise that all known things with A, B, and C have D also warrants the general conclusion that *all* things having A, B, and C probably have D. Since this general conclusion inferred by inductive generalization logically implies the more specific conclusion inferred by analogy, the latter form of inference is unnecessary: we can get the same result by a combination of induction and deduction.

Although the kind of analogical reasoning allowed by strict empiricists is, for them, logically redundant, they may still agree that it is a useful form of reasoning, which may be extremely convenient for some purposes. Their point in emphasizing its logical redundancy is that the conclusions it warrants are always capable of justification by the basic methods they officially accept. Analogy is therefore acceptable to them as a *derivative* form of inference, one owing its credentials to the logically prior forms of deduction and induction. The derivative status accorded to analogical inference has always been implicit in the pronouncements of orthodox empiricists; it is even implicit in Hume's famous remark that our experience of a constant conjunction between

---

* As in the case of induction, the premise that m/n things known to have A, B, and C also have D will support an appropriate statistical conclusion. In this case it may take the form of "the probability that an unexamined thing having A, B, and C will also have D is m/n." Analogical arguments with statistical premises are not mentioned in this text because the relation between induction and analogy, given strict empiricist assumptions, can be adequately understood without reference to them.

As and Bs leads us to form the belief that A is the cause of B, or that *all As* are conjoined with Bs, and *consequently to expect* (that is, to infer by analogy) that the next As we encounter will also be conjoined with Bs.

If this traditional empiricist approach to analogical reasoning is accepted, its use in justifying our common beliefs about other people's experiences must be rejected. The new empiricists emphatically endorse this consequence, arguing that the analogical argument for other experiences is not only untenable but fatal for our philosophical understanding. As they see it, in appearing to offer sound evidence for conjectures about completely unobservable items called "other persons' experiences," that argument hides the fundamental confusion that prompts Hume's alleged problem in the first place. This deep-seated confusion is contained in the traditional idea that a man's knowledge of his own experience has a purely subjective basis and that it makes sense to conceive of his feelings and thoughts in total abstraction from his behavior or situation in life. When the confusion inherent in this old idea is brought clearly into view, the emptiness of Hume's problem will be as unmistakable as the invalidity of the analogical argument used to solve it.

It was noted earlier in this chapter that recent empiricists commonly accept a modified form of Hume's principle that every legitimate idea must ultimately be derived from impressions. This principle has been turned against Hume on the question of subjective experiences, and it is therefore important for us to understand the new form it takes. Where Hume spoke of ideas, today's empiricists speak of words, and his principle for legitimate ideas has thus been transformed into a principle of meaning for descriptive words. According to this new principle, every meaningful descriptive expression must be either ostensively definable or definable in relation to other words that can be ostensively defined. To understand this new principle we must consequently understand what an ostensive definition is.

A word like "red" is not thought to be verbally definable; we are taught its meaning by having our attention directed to the color it stands for. If we have never experienced this color, we cannot hope to understand what the word means. An ostensive definition is the method by which the meaning of such words is conveyed; it is a form of definition by example. If I am asked to define the word "mauve," the most I can say is something like "It is a shade of purple"; to give its exact meaning I must point out examples of the color. In doing this, I shall be giving an ostensive definition. Words so defined correspond to Hume's simple ideas, whereas words capable of verbal definition correspond to his complex ideas. His principle that complex ideas must ultimately be analyzable into simple ideas is then transformed into the principle that verbally defined descriptive words must ultimately be definable by words that can be defined ostensively.

Empiricists have insisted on this principle as a means of describing the ultimate relation between words and the world. Ostensive definition establishes the basic tie between language and reality, and a verbally defined word owes its entire reference to the simple, ostensively defined expressions that explain its meaning. To understand a descriptive word one must therefore understand the situations in reality to which certain ostensive words correctly apply. As far as descriptive *statements* are concerned, the principle requires that we understand the conditions in experience that would make them true. It is because of the latter requirement that the empiricist's principle has come to be known as "the principle of verification." If we do not know which conditions in experience would verify the truth of a descriptive statement, we cannot, given this principle, claim to know what it asserts.

For the new empiricists, ostensive definition is a public activity whose general aim is to direct attention to something open to inspection by other members of one's linguistic community. This is regarded as a corollary of their view that the meaning of a word is a purely conventional matter and that its correct use must be amenable to community appraisal. Thus, Hume's idea that basic descriptive words apply to subjective experience is emphatically repudiated by the new empiricists; for them, basic descriptive words necessarily apply to phenomena open to public scrutiny. Since in their view defined words must be capable of elucidation by basic words whose meanings are given ostensively, they are committed to the idea that meaningful descriptive discourse necessarily concerns publicly accessible phenomena.

Consider the words we use for feelings such as pain. How are these words defined? Most often, ostensively. To teach someone what "pain" means you show him cases of people in pain; in doing this, you direct attention to a distinctive kind of human behavior. He will not, of course, learn to apply the word to himself by observing his own behavior; rather, he forms a *habit* of spontaneously using the word when he happens to be in pain. Nevertheless, it is on the basis of his behavior that his teachers determine whether his habit of responding with "I am in pain" is correctly established; in this sense even his use of the word "pain" in reference to himself is ultimately based on pain behavior. Since the correct use of all sensation words is ultimately determined behaviorally, it must be part of their meaning that they are correctly applied to people who display a specific form of behavior. The connection between distinctive pain behavior and the state of being in pain cannot, then, be purely synthetic nor can it be known only by experimental reasoning. It is known a priori. Since Hume's problem about the sensations of others was generated from the assumption that the connection is synthetic, it follows that Hume's problem is unwarranted.

The idea that words such as "pain" involve a tacit reference to observable behavior is not unreasonable, but it prompts the following line of objection: "I grant that the state of pain is a complex one involving a tendency to behave in a certain way. But surely this complex state includes, at least as a part of it, a subjective feeling—the feeling of being in pain. It is easy to see how the observation of behavior can prove that the behavioral aspects of the complex state of pain are present in another person, but how can it possibly prove that the state's subjective aspect is *also* present in him? This is really the basis of Hume's problem, and the argument just given does not solve this difficulty at all."

It is at this point that the verification principle is introduced, for the new empiricist is likely to reply: "What are you talking about? What do you *mean* in speaking of a 'subjective aspect'? If you are not referring to something publicly observable, you are

not making sense. I can understand you if you speak of the observable state of being in pain, but when you insist that you
are referring to something that cannot possibly be observed, you
make no sense to me at all."

When empiricists make this kind of response, they are implicitly defending a view known as "philosophical behaviorism."
This view is a cousin of phenomenalism; it might even be called
"phenomenalism of the mental." In effect, it attempts to reduce
mental states to their observable appearances. Since we cannot, on
strict empiricist principles, even make sense of something we cannot possibly observe, we must regard mental states as "constructs" out of behavior. This idea might be expressed by saying
that intelligible discourse concerning feelings and thoughts must
be understood as referring to special patterns of behavior or to
dispositions (tendencies, propensities, states of readiness) to behave
in certain ways under various conditions. It may be admitted
that the forms of behavior associated with particular mentalistic
words cannot be precisely described, but this shows only that the
words in question have a somewhat vague meaning. It does not
show that behaviorism is erroneous.

Although behaviorism of this kind is a decidedly bizarre view
hardly more credible to common sense than phenomenalism, it
has been widely accepted in recent years. One reason for its popu-
larity is that, like phenomenalism, it promises a means of solving
important philosophical difficulties—specifically, skeptical difficulties about our knowledge of other minds. Another reason for its
success is the extreme difficulty of showing a behaviorist that his
view ignores something real and important. As soon as one mentions any purely subjective element in sensory experience, the
behaviorist will profess an utter inability to understand what one
is saying. His inability to understand such speech, even if entirely
genuine, does not of course prove that the speech is incompre-
hensible. But at a time when the basic principles of empiricism
are widely accepted as obvious truths, it is difficult to demonstrate that the behaviorist's attitude is certainly mistaken or that
an acceptable alternative to his position can be found.

The difficulty of avoiding behaviorism on strict new-empiricist
principles can be seen by reference to the ostensibly very reason-

able position of P. F. Strawson, an influential recent writer. According to him, the behaviorist is undoubtedly correct on one point: the behavior we rely on in ascribing conscious states to others cannot always be merely contingently associated with those states; it must, at least sometimes, provide "criteria of a logically adequate kind" for ascribing those states to others. But this does not imply, Strawson insists, that there is nothing more to a conscious state than behavior or a tendency to behave in a certain way. Indeed, if there were not a subjective aspect to a conscious state, no one would ever have entertained the idea that the mental states of others are perhaps unknowable. Strawson illustrates his view by considering the concept of depression:

> We speak of behaving in a depressed way (of depressed behaviour) and we also speak of feeling depressed (of a feeling of depression). One is inclined to argue that feelings can be felt but not observed, and behavior can be observed but not felt, and that therefore there must be room to drive in a logical wedge. But the concept of depression spans the place where one wants to drive it in. We might say: in order for there to be such a concept as that of X's depression, . . . the concept must cover both what is felt, but not observed, by X, and what may be observed, but not felt, by others than X. . . . To refuse to accept this is to refuse to accept the structure of the language in which we talk about depression.[3]

Strawson's position is this. We possess concepts such as depression, which we apply on occasion both to ourselves and to others. Although these concepts arise in a social context, they are not purely behavioral; they refer to complex states that involve feelings as well as behavior. Skepticism is unwarranted because it is part of the logic of these concepts that they are correctly applied on the basis of observable behavior, and behaviorism is unwarranted because these concepts involve an inescapable reference to subjective feelings. Both these extreme positions therefore result from ignoring a crucial aspect of our mentalistic concepts. If the total implications of these concepts are kept in view, they cannot be used in formulating a position that undermines what Hume would call our customary beliefs about the mental.

The crucial weakness in Strawson's position is best brought out by an analogy. Consider the word "lunatic." As this word was originally used, it carried the implication that a form of mental disorder, "lunacy," was brought about by the influence of the moon. Given this original usage, one could not consistently say that a man's lunacy has nothing to do with the moon. To put the point in Strawson's terms, the original concept of lunacy does not allow one to drive in a logical wedge between a certain form of mental disorder and the influence of the moon, because the concept "spans the place" where one might want to drive in the wedge. To use the word in its original sense, we must accept a certain general assumption; if we refuse to accept this assumption, we refuse to accept "the structure of the language" in which people used to talk about lunacy.

Today, of course, virtually no one is prepared to use "lunacy" in its original sense; the assumption on which it was based is no longer regarded as acceptable. But what about the assumption on which, according to Strawson, our present use of "depression" is based? Is this assumption acceptable? Are we entitled to assume that something publicly unobservable, a so-called feeling of depression, *generally accompanies* the depressed behavior we can observe in those around us? To raise this question is not to deny that we customarily make this assumption and that as ordinary men we have no doubts about its acceptability. Even Hume would grant these facts without reservation. The point of the question is rather to elicit the grounds, if any, on which the assumption is based. Is there any way of proving that the assumption is true?

From what was said earlier about the basic principles of the new empiricism, it is clear that the assumption in question must be regarded as groundless and even nonsensical. It involves a crucial reference, after all, to something publicly unobservable (namely, a so-called feeling of depression). And if introspection is disallowed as a basic means of obtaining genuine knowledge, there is no way, on strict empiricist principles, of defending any claim about unobservable feelings. If we take these principles in earnest, a behavioristic interpretation of thoughts and feelings is inescapable. Strawson's interpretation is admittedly far closer to our customary beliefs, but it cannot be accepted as sound unless the basic assumptions of the new empiricism are radically revised.

It was mentioned earlier that behaviorism might be termed a "phenomenalism of the mental." We might note here that the principles leading to behaviorism require a further kind of phenomenalism, one concerning scientific objects. In rejecting phenomenalism proper, the new empiricist sought to defend our instinctive belief in the external world. But the external world that concerned him was a world of publicly observable objects, such as trees and houses. The theoretical scientist is apparently committed to a very different external world, one consisting of individually unobservable micro-objects, such as electrons, neutrons, and protons. Since these alleged entities cannot possibly be observed, their existence as independent objects cannot be defended on strict empiricist principles; there is simply no way of establishing a correlation between them and things (such as tracks in the Wilson cloud chamber) that we can observe. Given the principle of verification, this implies that discourse about such entities must be meaningless unless we can interpret it as a kind of shorthand for discourse about observables. To offer such an interpretation is, however, to embrace a phenomenalism of scientific objects. A phenomenalism of this kind is unlikely to be convincing to men working with the electron microscope, but it seems to be the only way of squaring the physicist's claims with the basic commitments of the new empiricism.

4. A Final Estimate of Empiricism

The strength of empiricism lies in its rigorous demands for legitimate knowledge. In restricting a priori knowledge to relations between ideas, it requires all knowledge of matters of fact and existence to be founded on observation, memory, and inductive generalization. This approach quickly undermines the pretensions of armchair physics and speculative philosophy, but in doing so it inevitably renders doubtful some of the most confidently held beliefs of science and everyday life. In the traditional form developed by Hume, the approach tends toward solipsism, thus destroying, as Hume remarked, virtually "all assurance and conviction." In its recent form, it threatens our common beliefs about subjective experience (our own as well as those of others), and it undermines the literal force of scientific claims about theoretical entities such as hydrogen atoms. Hence, the strength of empiricism is also, paradoxically, its weakness. Its standards for legitimate knowledge and meaningful discourse are so stringent that in disallowing the extravagant claims of dogma, faith, and fancy it tends to reduce our intellectual horizons to a tiny sphere, the sphere of the observable. Empiricists have quarreled about the precise contents of this sphere, but whatever it is taken to include, something important seems to be left out as unknowable or even inconceivable.

STUDY QUESTIONS

1. What is phenomenalism? What epistemological problem was it designed to solve? Was it successful in solving this problem? Explain.

2. Evaluate the following claim: "Although phenomenalism may be counted a failure as a means of solving a basic epistemological problem, it may nevertheless be a true metaphysical theory."

3. Critics of Hume have argued that a fundamental flaw in his philosophy was his conclusion that we strictly observe images or mental representations rather than external objects. What argument led Hume to his conclusion, and how has this argument been criticized by Hume's philosophical opponents? Is their criticism valid?

4. Descartes observed that there are "no certain marks" by which dreaming can be distinguished from waking experience. This observation has recently been attacked, chiefly on two grounds. What are these grounds? Are they acceptable?

5. What was Wittgenstein's argument for the claim that we cannot make sense of "knowledge" or "pain" on a purely subjective basis? In his view what is the proper touchstone of empirical truth?

6. What are the basic epistemological tenets of the new empiricism? How do these tenets differ from those of Hume?

7. To what extent does the new empiricist avoid Hume's specific

problems regarding minds? What aspect of Hume's problem cannot be avoided by the new empiricist?

8. What is the analogical argument for the existence of another person's experience? On what inductive principle is the argument based? How might this principle be defended?

9. To what extent can unqualified analogical reasoning yield conclusions contrary to the commitments of orthodox empiricists? How do such empiricists limit the applicability of analogical reasoning?

10. According to strict empiricists, analogical reasoning is a *derivative* form of inference. Explain.

11. What is ostensive definition? What role does this notion play in empiricist theories of meaning?

12. What is philosophical behaviorism? On what grounds is this position defended?

13. How does P. F. Strawson attempt to avoid the extreme positions of skepticism and philosophical behaviorism? What difficulties are involved in Strawson's procedure?

14. Formulate in your own words the leading strengths and weaknesses of empiricism as an epistemological position.

SUGGESTIONS FOR FURTHER READING

On the topic of phenomenalism good general discussions may be found in John Hospers, *An Introduction to Philosophical Analysis*, 2nd ed. (Englewood Cliffs, N.J.: Prentice-Hall, 1967), pp. 530–565, and in C. H. Whiteley, *An Introduction to Metaphysics* (London: Methuen, 1950), Chaps. 6–7. Classic sources of phenomenalist ideas are George Berkeley, *Three Dialogues Between Hylas and Phylonous* (originally published in 1710), available in numerous editions; David Hume, *A Treatise of Human Nature* (1739), also available in numerour editions; and John Stuart Mill, *An Examination of Sir William Hamilton's Philosophy* (London: Longmans, Green, 1865), Chaps. 11–12. Important twentieth-century defenses of phenomenalist positions may be found in Bertrand Russell, *Our Knowledge of the External World* (London: Allen & Unwin, 1914); H. H. Price, *Hume's Theory of the External World* (Oxford: Clarendon Press, 1940); C. I.

Lewis, *An Analysis of Knowledge and Valuation* (LaSalle, Ill.: Open Court, 1946), esp. Chaps. 7–8; A. J. Ayer, *Foundations of Empirical Knowledge* (New York: Macmillan, 1940) and *Philosophical Essays* (New York: Macmillan, 1955), esp. the essay "Phenomenalism," pp. 125–166.

Influential essays critical of phenomenalism are included in a recent paperback edited by Robert J. Swartz, *Perceiving, Sensing, Knowing* (Garden City, N.Y.: Anchor Books, 1965). Further criticism may be found in Wilfrid Sellars, *Science, Perception, and Reality* (London: Routledge & Kegan Paul, 1964), Chap. 3, and in Bruce Aune, *Knowledge, Mind, and Nature* (New York: Random House, 1967), Chap. 3. Full annotated bibliographies concerned with phenomenalism and related subjects are contained in Paul Edwards and Arthur Pap, eds., *A Modern Introduction to Philosophy*, 2nd. ed. (New York: Free Press, 1965), pp. 583–590, and in R. J. Hirst, *Perception and the External World* (New York: Macmillan, 1965), pp. 303–310.

Essays concerned with the proper objects of perception are legion, and the bibliographies in the volumes by Edwards and Pap, *op. cit.*, and by Hirst, *op. cit.*, list the most significant. Three especially influential discussions are the following, all of which are reprinted in Swartz, *op cit.*: Winston Barnes, "The Myth of Sense Data"; Roderick Chisholm, "The Theory of Appearing"; and Anthony Quinton, "The Problem of Perception."

The marked difference, alleged in this text, between dreaming and waking experience was emphasized by the late J. L. Austin in influential lectures given at Oxford and other universities; the lectures are now available as reconstructed from Austin's notes by G. J. Warnock in Austin, *Sense and Sensibilia* (Oxford: Clarendon Press, 1962). Another recent but highly controversial discussion of the distinction is Norman Malcolm, *Dreaming* (London: Routledge & Kegan Paul, 1959).

Ludwig Wittgenstein's revolutionary approach to the problems of epistemology is recorded in his posthumous *Philosophical Investigations*, G. E. M. Anscombe, tr. (Oxford: Blackwell, 1953). A very useful collection of articles concerned with Wittgenstein's difficult book is George Pitcher, ed., *Wittgenstein: The Philosophical Investigations* (Garden City, N.Y.: Anchor Books, 1966). This volume contains a comprehensive bibliography on Wittgenstein and includes essays by Anthony Quinton and Norman Malcolm, which form a very helpful introduction to Wittgenstein's later philosophy.

A now classic work in the spirit of the new empiricism is Gilbert

Ryle, *The Concept of Mind* (London: Hutchinson, 1949). It is in this book that the conception of a man's mind as chiefly involving abilities and capacities is most forcefully developed. Austin, *Sense and Sensibilia, op. cit.*, is also written in the spirit of the new empiricism, as are the essays by Norman Malcolm collected in his *Knowledge and Certainty: Essays and Lectures* (Englewood Cliffs, N.J.: Prentice-Hall, 1964). Aspects of the new empiricism are critically discussed by Bruce Aune, *op. cit.*, esp. Chaps. 1–7.

An exact formulation of the principle of analogy and an astute account of its application to the problem of other minds may be found in Bertrand Russell, *Human Knowledge: Its Scope and Limits* (London: Allen & Unwin, 1948), pp. 501–505. The most influential objections to the argument from analogy are set forth in Norman Malcolm's essay "Knowledge of Other Minds," reprinted in his *Knowledge and Certainty, op. cit.*, pp. 130–140. For a general discussion of analogical reasoning not limited by strict empiricist principles, see Irving Copi, *Introducton to Logic* (New York: Macmillan, 1961), pp. 337–343.

Philosophical behaviorism is explicitly defended in C. G. Hempel, "The Logical Analysis of Psychology," in H. Feigl and W. Sellars, eds., *Readings in Philosophical Analysis* (New York: Appleton-Century-Crofts, 1949), pp. 373–384, and in Rudolf Carnap, "Psychology and Physical Language," in A. J. Ayer, ed., *Logical Positivism* (New York: Free Press, 1959), pp. 165–198. Gilbert Ryle, *The Concept of Mind, op. cit.*, is also generally interpreted as a defense of philosophical behaviorism. A comprehensive bibliography containing entries on philosophical behaviorism may be found in Edwards and Pap, *op. cit.*, pp. 266–278.

Instrumentalism, or phenomenalism of scientific objects, is usefully discussed in two books by J. J. C. Smart: *Philosophy and Scientific Realism* (London: Routledge & Kegan Paul, 1963), Chap. 2, and *Between Science and Philosophy: An Introduction to the Philosophy of Science* (New York: Random House, 1968), Chap. 5.

CHAPTER IV

Pragmatism
and A Priori Knowledge

Pragmatism is justly regarded as a distinctively American philosophy. It originated with the American Charles Sanders Peirce (1839–1914), had William James (1842–1910) and John Dewey (1859–1952) as early adherents, and is still a dominant force on the American scene. Although its originator, Peirce, was one of the most original and profound of all philosophers, we shall not rely on his work for our understanding of pragmatism. Unlike Descartes and Hume, Peirce was a difficult, technical, and frequently very obscure writer. Since recent philosophers have also made important contributions to pragmatic philosophy, we shall move directly to the present and offer an idealized account of the general position that is now associated with the name of pragmatism. This approach will allow us to formulate an especially clear alternative to the rival positions of rationalism and empiricism.

1. The Pragmatic Approach to the A Priori

It is only in recent years that the pragmatist's approach to the a priori has achieved its clearest formulation. The distinctive features of this approach are best understood in relation to the pragmatist's critique of the basic claims of rationalism and empiricism. The general strategy of his critique involves two important steps. The first is to show that, appearances to the contrary, the rationalist and empiricist positions on the a priori are fundamentally the same. The second step is to show that this common position of rationalism and empiricism is indefensible.

As we have seen in discussing Descartes, the rationalist holds that the most important a priori truths are synthetic and known intuitively. The empiricist emphatically denies this, saying that all a priori truths are analytic. By subjecting the notion of analytic truth to searching analysis, the pragmatist attempts to show that in spite of the empiricist's vehement denials, the latter's position on basic analytic truths is not appreciably different from that of the rationalist. Ultimately, both positions are forced to appeal to an indefensible intuition.

In order to extend the scope of analyticity to encompass statements lacking subject-predicate form the empiricist generally accepts Kant's definition in the *Prolegomena:*

(1) "A statement S is analytically true" = df. "the denial of S, or not-S, is self-contradictory."

This definition immediately prompts the questions "What is a self-contradiction?" and "How is such a contradiction recognized?" To avoid an immediate appeal to an intuition of contradictoriness, or to one's presumed inability to *conceive* the possibility of a statement's truth, the empiricist introduces the notion of an *explicit* contradiction. A statement is explicitly contradictory when it has the form "S and not-S." Such statements are regarded as obviously false because they explicitly assert and, at the same time, deny the very same thing.

This maneuver obviously makes clear the notion of a contradiction, but it is not sufficient to clarify the empiricist's criterion of analyticity. The reason for this is simply that the negation of *no* analytic statement is an explicit contradiction. Take, for example, the simple case of "not-(S and not-S)." This compound statement is analytic if anything is; yet its explicit denial is not "S and not-S" but "Not-(not-(S and not-S))." It may be argued, of course, that the last two statements are obviously equivalent, but the same cannot be said for "S and not-S" and "not-(A vixen is a female fox)," even though the latter statement is universally regarded as the negation of an analytic truth.

To avoid this kind of difficulty the empiricist introduces a fur-

ther notion, that of an *implicit* contradiction. An implicit contradiction is a statement that implies an explicit contradiction. Since
the denials of analytic truths are not explicit contradictons, the
empiricist uses this new notion to improve his criterion:

(2)   "S is analytically true" = df. "the denial of S is an implicit contradiction."

This improved criterion obviously does not face the difficulty previously mentioned, but it raises further problems in its turn.
The most pressing of these problems concerns the notion of
implication. Since an implicit contradiction is defined as something *implying* an explicit contradiction, the acceptability of the
new criterion will obviously depend on what is meant by the term
"implies."

According to the usage of most empiricists, "implies" has two
relevant senses, one broader than the other. In the broadest sense,
"implies" is equivalent to "analytically entails." This broad sense
of the word cannot help us to evaluate the criterion above, because
"P analytically entails Q" is commonly explained as meaning
that the statement "If P then Q" is analytically true. Since
the notion of analytic truth is what the criterion above purports
to clarify, this broad sense of "implies" is useless for our purpose.
If we are to elucidate the notion of analytic truth by reference to
"implication," we must therefore consider the narrower sense
of the word.

In the narrower sense, "implies" has the sense of "logically implies." Unlike analytic entailment generally, logical implication is
commonly understood as a purely formal relation. If a statement
S logically implies a statement P, it does so by virtue of the laws
of logic, which are extremely general and concern a statement's
form rather than its specific content. Perhaps the simplest example
of a logical law is the one implicit in the empiricist's definition of
analytic truth, namely, the law of contradiction. According to this
law, every statement of the form "S and not-S" must be false.
This law is a purely *formal* one in the sense that it holds for
every statement S. This kind of form involved is also *logical*
form, because it is defined by the presence of the logical words
"and" and "not." These logical words form a distinctive pattern

in this case, "——— and not ———," and all instances of this pattern are declared false by the law in question.

The simplest cases of logical implication are instances of the elementary laws of logic. Examples of such laws are "If *P*, then *P*"; "If *P* and *Q*, then *P*"; and "If *P*, then P or *Q*." More complicated cases of logical implication are inferred from elementary laws by logically valid rules of inference. An example of such a rule of inference is *modus ponens:* "From premises 'P' and 'If *P*, then *Q*,' one may infer '*Q*.'" This rule is logically valid in the sense that it allows only true conclusions to be drawn from true premises; this is ensured by the fact that its corresponding conditional statement, "If *P*, and if *P* then *Q*, then *Q*," is an elementary truth of logic.

Assuming that we can identify the basic laws and rules of logic, we can easily characterize the narrower sense of "implies":

(3)   "A statement *S* logically implies a statement *Q*" = df. "the hypothetical statement 'If *S*, then *Q*' is either an instance of an elementary law of logic or can be inferred from such laws by valid logical rules."

This narrow sense of "implies" is not adequate, however, to clarify the empiricist's improved criterion (2), since some statements universally accepted as analytic are not formal truths. Although the denials of such statements may be held to imply contradictions, the implication in question is not purely formal or logical. To obtain the requisite contradiction we must also employ definitions of the nonlogical words the statement involves.

Consider the statement "If someone is a father, he is a parent." This is universally allowed as analytic, but it is obviously not a formal truth, and its denial does not itself logically imply a contradiction. To get a contradiction from its denial we must rely on the definition of the word "father." If we take this word as meaning "male parent," we can then reexpress the original statement as "If someone is a male parent, he is a male parent." The latter statement *is* logically true, and its denial does logically imply a contradiction.

The treatment just given to the statement "If someone is a father, he is a parent" illuminates the broad sense of "implies" equivalent to "analytically entails." This sense may be explicitly defined as follows:

(4)   "S analytically entails P" = df. "S, together with adequate definitions of the nonlogical expressions of S and P, logically implies P."

If we understand "implies" in this broad sense, the empiricist's improved criterion(2) seems to provide a reasonable analysis of the notion of analytic truth. Expressed more explicitly, the criterion amounts to the following:

(5)   "S is analytically true" = df. "the denial of S, together with adequate definitions of the nonlogical expressions occurring in it, logically implies a statement of the form 'P and not-P.' "

Logical implication is thus the empiricist's basic notion, and when this notion is supplemented by the idea of an adequate definition, it permits a fairly straightforward definition of analytic truth.

Since the notion of an analytic truth is based on the idea of logical implication, the pragmatist's attack on the empiricist's conception of a priori truth is directed to this basic idea. How, in general, the pragmatist wants to know, does one determine whether one statement logically implies another? And can this be determined without a rationalist appeal to intuition?

Given our definition (3) of logical implication, we can easily answer part of this question. We can say that a statement P logically implies a statement Q when, and only when, the hypothetical "If P, then Q" is either an elementary law of logic or a statement that can be inferred from such laws by a logically valid rule of inference. If we can identify elementary laws of logic and valid principles of inference, we can therefore determine, at least in principle, whether one statement logically implies another. This does not, unfortunately, answer the pragmatist's entire question; it does not tell us how we identify elementary logical laws and determine that they are true. Obviously, we cannot say that elementary logical laws are merely the simplest cases of analytic truths, for this would be arguing in a circle. Our definition of "analytically true" is based on the idea of a law of logic, and it cannot therefore be used to justify the truth of such a law.

It was pointed out above that logical laws are extremely general and concern a statement's form rather than its specific content. Logical laws are said to be formal truths, defined by their distinctive pattern of logical words. Thus, any compound statement of the form "not-(S and not-S)" is supposed to be a logical truth, no matter what "S" might be. This idea has been used by the contemporary logician W. V. O. Quine as a means of identifying logical truths: they are simply those true statements in which only logical words appear "essentially"—that is, those statements, like "not-(Grass is green and not-(Grass is green))," whose truth hinges entirely on the pattern of their constituent logical words and would remain true if their nonlogical words were uniformly replaced by others.[1] The statement just given is logically true in this sense because it would remain true if "Grass is green" were uniformly replaced by the sentence "$2 + 2 = 4$." The result of the substitution would be "not-($2 + 2 = 4$ and not $- (2 + 2 = 4)$)" —and this is also an instance of the law of contradiction.

If we assume that we can tell a logical word when we see one, it might seem possible to rely on Quine's idea and to argue that certain statements are logically true because their truth hinges entirely on the presence of their constituent logical words. This procedure undoubtedly works for the identification of derivative logical truths, but unfortunately it cannot help us identify those that are basic or elementary. If we are to prove that a statement is true because of the pattern of its logical words, we shall have to employ an *argument*. But an argument can show only that a conclusion is as good as the premises from which it is inferred. If we do not have premises whose truth is certain, the truth of our conclusion must remain undetermined. When, however, we are concerned with what we regard as basic or elementary logical truths, we cannot possibly hope to find more fundamental premises from which their truth can be inferred. This is, indeed, a matter of definition. Anything whose truth can be established by argument is a *derivative* truth; we know that it is true only because we know that something else is true. Basic or elementary truths do not owe their truth to something more basic; for this reason it is out of the question to try to establish their truth by some kind of argument.

If we cannot, then, rely on inference to establish the truth of the basic laws of logic, how can we possibly know that the laws commonly accepted as basic are true? It is at this point that the rationalist stresses the inescapable soundness of his root contention. According to him, elementary laws can be known to be true by immediate intuition—and this is the only way their truth can possibly be known. His axiom is: If anything can be proved by argument or inference, something must be known directly and without argument. It is only in this direct, intuitive manner that the basic principles and laws needed for all argument can possibly be known. As far as basic logical principles are concerned, their truth is simply obvious to any mature, attentive mind; no rational being could possibly doubt their intrinsic acceptability.

The last idea—that no rational being could possibly doubt the elementary laws of logic—has the weight of history behind it, and it certainly appears to support the rationalist's position. The standard objection to his reliance on intuition is that rival intuitions are always possible and that intuition cannot itself decide which intuitions are correct. But rival intuitions do not seem possible, the rationalist will say, regarding the basic laws of logic. As Aristotle argued in ancient times, these laws cannot be doubted because they are presupposed in all rational thought, even the kind of thought called "doubting." If you doubt that P, it is because you see at least some plausibility in the idea that not-P and assume that P and not-P are incompatible. And to assume this is to accept the law of contradiction as sound.

The impossibility, here alleged, of doubting the elementary laws of logic, has in practice been stressed by empiricists as well as rationalists. But the empiricist's practice in this regard is just a symptom, the pragmatist insists, of the underlying identity in these traditionally opposing views. It was, after all, a cardinal tenet of Descartes' position that indubitability is the basic criterion of truth; if the empiricist appeals to this notion in support of the truth of basic logical laws, he is simply falling into the rationalist's hands without realizing it. The fact that the empiricist does not like or use the *word* "intuition" is not sufficient to distinguish his essential views from those of his opponents. To rely on indubitability as the mark of basic truth is to accept the key claim of rationalism; this holds good even if some other terminology is preferred, such as "directly evident," "obvious on inspection," or simply "self-evident."

For the pragmatist, these considerations make it clear that the rationalist and the empiricist hold the same basic position regarding the justification of primitive a priori truths; their major difference is merely one of terminology and scope. The rationalist simply finds *more* principles self-evident or indubitable than the empiricist will allow. The latter is content to award this status to the basic laws of logic; the former extends it to nonformal truths such as Descartes' principle that existence is a perfection or that there must be as much reality in a total cause as is contained, formally and objectively, in its effect. Aside from scope and terminology, the two positions are identical on the nature and ground of a priori truth.

Having argued that, when pressed, the rationalist and empiricist take essentially the same position on the a priori, the pragmatist has completed the first step of his critique. His second step is to show that this common position is untenable.

We have already noted the standard objection to rationalism—namely, that self-evidence, indubitability, or even universal agreement by attentive minds cannot possibly *guarantee* that a statement is true. The pragmatist strongly endorses this objection, but he also thinks that positive grounds can be given for questioning the absolute certainty of any statement whatever, even those formulating the basic laws of logic. To appreciate his position on this matter we shall consider three of the traditional laws of thought: the law of the excluded middle, the law of contradiction, and the law of identity.

The law of the excluded middle can be formulated as the claim that every statement is either true or false. To rebut this claim it is sufficient to find a statement for which the law fails. The following, call it "S," appears to be such a statement:

This statement is false.

The law of the excluded middle fails for the statement S because the claim that this statement is either true or false leads to a contradiction. Suppose, first, that S is true. Since S is the very statement that it, S, declares to be false, the assumption that it is true leads to the conclusion that it is also false. Suppose, on the other hand, that S is false. On this assumption S must also be true, since it says that it is false and, on our assumption, does so falsely. Thus, the idea that S is either true or false leads to a contradiction and must be rejected. This seems to demonstrate that the law of the excluded middle is not universally valid.

Philosophers who defend the law of the excluded middle are, of course, aware of such statements as S. They do not, however, regard them as refuting the law, since they hold them to be meaningless or else not genuine statements. Unfortunately, these means of defending the law do not have much plausibility. Not only does S itself seem to be a perfectly meaningful and genuine statement, but there are many other statements far less peculiar than S that also falsify the law. Consider, for example, the statement "The statement on page 85 is false." There is nothing intrinsically puzzling about this statement; yet if it happens to appear by itself on page 85, we could use this fact to obtain the same sort of contradiction we inferred from the statement S.

It is not merely self-reference that raises difficulties for the law of the excluded middle. Problems also rise from the occurrence in statements of special names and descriptions and from the ascription to subjects of inappropriate characteristics. Consider the statement "Zeus is insane." This is certainly not a true statement, but need we infer that it is false if Zeus does not exist? Some philosophers would say "No"; for them, statements referring to nonexistent things are typically neither true nor false. Consider also the statement "The square root of 4 is asleep." Is this either true or false if taken literally? Again, many philosophers would say "No"; in their opinion the statement lacks truth value because the predicate "is asleep" can be truly or falsely applied only to animals. If they are right about this and right about the statement concerning Zeus, it would then appear that the law of the excluded middle has countless exceptions.

Although the law of contradiction may seem far less dubious than the law of the excluded middle, the two laws are demonstrably equivalent in standard systems of logic and will fail for the very same statements. Consider first the statement S, "This statement is false." As was shown above, if S is true it is also false, and if it is false it is also true. Hence, if it has any truth value at all, it is quite possible for it to be both true and false, which is incompatible with the law of contradiction. Now consider the other two statements, "Zeus is insane" and "The square root of 4 is asleep." According to the law of contradiction, every compound statement of the form "P and not-P" must be false. But if "P" is replaced by either of the two statements above, then, assuming that these statements lack truth value, the resulting conjunctions —"Zeus is insane, and it is not the case that Zeus is insane" and "The square root of 4 is asleep, and it is not the case that the square root of 4 is asleep"—will also lack truth value. If this is so, however, the claim that these conjunctive statements must be false will then be erroneous, and the law of contradiction will fail.

The idea that the law of contradiction could fail for the cases just cited may be very surprising in view of the traditional assumption that we must presuppose this law in all our reasoning. This assumption is false, however; for we do not presuppose the law in the reasoning given above. In arguing that the schema "P and not-P" is not false for every statement, we need establish only that there is at least one statement P for which the conjunction "P and not-P" is not false. In arguing this way we must, of course, assume that "There is at least one statement P such that it is not false that P and not-P" is incompatible with "For every statement P, it is false that P and not-P." But the latter assumption is not the same as the law of contradiction. What we assume in the latter case is that *two particular statements* are incompatible—not that *every statement* is such that the conjunction of it and its negation must be false. This assumption concerning every statement is precisely what we wish to deny.

Now let us consider the law of identity. According to contemporary logical practice, this law may be formulated as "For every object x, x is identical with x." Using the symbol for equality in place of the expression "is identical with," we may ask whether it is indeed true that *everything* x is such that $x = x$. What about Zeus? Must we agree that Zeus = Zeus? If we accept a standard rule of modern logic, we may infer from "Zeus = Zeus" the conclusion "There is something identical with Zeus."

But Zeus does not exist. Given this, it seems false to say that there is something identical with him.

Consider next the statement "The present king of France is identical with the present king of France." According to Russell's influential analysis of the meaning of definite descriptions such as "the present king of France," the identity statement above is equivalent to the existential statement "There is exactly one king of France, and he is self-identical." But the claim that there is a present king of France is false. Hence, if Russell's theory of definitive descriptions is correct, the law of identity fails for such statments as "The present king of France = the present king of France." And if the statement "Zeus = Zeus" also implies that *there is* something identical with Zeus or that Zeus exists, the law of identity fails for this case as well.

Is it correct to interpret the cases above as refuting the law of identity? Contemporary logicians disagree on this point. Some hold that a statement of the form "$a = a$" is true only if "a exists" is true; others hold that "$a = a$" must be true, but that it does not imply that anything exists. What is the pragmatist's view of the matter? He will say that we can have it either way. Depending on the other logical principles we accept, we can either accept the law of identity in its most general form or restrict its application to objects that exist. This reference to our other logical principles is of crucial importance, because it is only with reference to other logical principles that the law of identity even makes sense.

The pragmatist's point can be explained as follows. If we allow the inference of "There is something $= a$" from "$a = a$," we must interpret identity as relating only to existent things; if we disallow this inference, we must intrepret identity in some other way. In either case the meaning we attach to "$a = a$" will be determined by the inferences we allow. Since it is strictly up to us to mean what we want by the expressions we use, we can either accept or reject a completely general statement of the law of identity. This point is of fundamental importance to the pragmatist's rejection of rationalism and empiricism, for both positions involve the assumption that a statement can be considered logically true or false in isolation from other statements. For the pragmatist, this idea is totally false: the question whether a statement is true or false can be answered only with reference to a *system* of other statements.

The last considerations throw important light on the pragmatist's attitude toward the laws of contradiction and the excluded middle. Although we were able to find apparent counterinstances to these laws, the pragmatist will agree that these instances do not actually require that we abandon the laws. We may, if we wish, reject such statements as "This statement is false" and "The square root of 4 is asleep" as illegitimate or meaningless; and we may declare that the statement "Zeus is insane" is false, even though Zeus does not exist. If we take these steps, we can continue to hold that the laws in question are sound: we can say that they hold for every statement we regard as *acceptable*. Our decision will be purely practical, however; it will not depend on a mysterious intuition of ultimate truth.

2. *Logic as the Ethics of Belief*

The contentions just made may seem less surprising if we note that logic is not, for the pragmatist, the theory of some abstract subject matter; it is rather the "ethics of belief." A man's beliefs and opinions are subject to logical criticism, just as his deeds are subject to moral criticism. A belief may be deemed right or wrong, depending on the available evidence; if a man holds one belief, it may be considered wrong (incorrect) for him to hold certain others. These logical (or epistemic) rights and wrongs are based on rules or standards of acceptable reasoning. The thoughts and opinions of a rational being are normally expect' d to be based on some kind of reasoning, and if his reasoning conforms to accepted standards it is said to be sound or correct. Formal logic is concerned with the most general and abstract features of acceptable reasoning; it lays down basic rules that should be followed in using such abstract, formal notions as *some, all, and, not,* and *if.*

In discussing the law of identity we observed that the meaning of a premise is largely determined by the inferences it warrants. Since it is ultimately up to us to mean what we want by the words we use, it is also up to us to decide which principles of inference we are prepared to use and to support. The rules of logic are distinctive in concerning the formal structure of acceptable inference; they specify the conclusions that may be drawn from premises of a certain abstract form. Like other rules of inference, these formal rules are something we are ultimately free to accept or to reject. We may or may not want to mean specific things by particular words, and we may or may not want to commit ourselves to certain general procedures in our reasoning.

As an illustration of the relation between the meaning of a word and an associated formal rule of inference, we might consider the following:

> From a premise of the form "*P and Q*" (for example, "It is raining *and* the streets are wet") one may draw the conclusion "P."

This rule expresses part of what is ordinarily meant by the logical word "and." There is obviously more to its meaning than what is given by this rule, but the rule unquestionably spells out an important element of the logical significance of the word. It is not necessary, of course, for us to use the word with this standard meaning; in fact, it is not necessary for us to use the word at all. We may rightly anticipate serious practical difficulties if we tried to avoid using any word in accordance with the rule above, but nevertheless such usage is not *forced* upon us.

The idea that we are free to choose certain meanings for our words and are therefore free to accept certain principles of inference is thus consistent with the fact that our choice may be advantageous or disastrous. A disastrous choice would be made if we chose rules that jointly allowed the inference of a contradiction. We may not have to agree that every statement of the form "*P and not-P*" is false, since it is possible, as we saw, that some statements of this form may reasonably be regarded as lacking in truth value. But we cannot allow such statements as true, for they would then say and unsay the same thing at the same time and thereby defeat the purposes of literal discourse. We must, consequently, be careful to choose a system of logical rules that is consistent, that is, one that does not permit the deduction of a contradiction.

It might be asked at this point, "But how are we to know whether a certain system of proposed logical rules is consistent in this sense?" The pragmatist's answer is that we shall know that our system is inconsistent if we discover that it generates a contradiction. If no contradiction is derived from a set of rules, it does not follow, of course, that no contradiction will ever be derived from it. Yet if our system has worked successfully in the past, we may come to have great faith in its consistency. We may, it is true, attempt to prove its consistency, but to do this we shall have to assume the consistency of some other system of rules. If we have only one basic system to work with, such a proof will not be possible.* In this case we shall have to work with what we have and be willing to modify our system should trouble arise. In the meantime, our chief guide to the consistency of our system is our past success in working with it.

At this stage in the history of logic there are numerous systems of logic whose consistency is not in doubt. Some of these systems differ significantly from others. Different logicians recommend different systems and back their recommendations by practical considerations. Aside from the obvious consideration of having a system that is comprehensive enough to be useful, one of the great merits of standard systems is their simplicity. It is on this ground that logicians such as Quine hold to the law of the excluded middle and regard every statement, including "Zeus is insane" and "The square root of 4 is asleep," as either true or false. Other logicians refuse to accept the law in its usual form, arguing that it is more in line with our everyday practice to regard some statements as neither true nor false. According to these men, it is preferable to say that the question whether some statements are

---

* Technically, this is misleading. If we have one system of explicit rules, implicitly we also have an infinite hierarchy of further systems, each of which is, in effect, a replica of our original one. As we make explicit these implicit rules, we may use the second system to prove the consistency of the first, the third system to prove the consistency of the second, and so on. This procedure is not strictly circular, since each system of the hierarchy is distinguishable from the others. Yet if we were ever in doubt about the consistency of our original system, this means of resolving our doubt could scarcely be taken seriously.

true or false simply does not arise except under special conditions. An example of such a statement is "Zeus is insane." Unless it is assumed that there is such a being as Zeus, the question whether it is true or false that Zeus is insane does not arise.

Similarly, although most logicians regard self-referential statements such as "This statement (or the statement on page 85) is false" as objectionable for reasons already noted, some logicians insist that self-referential statements are necessary and important for certain subjects. The logician Frederick B. Fitch has argued, for example, that philosophers have a special and legitimate concern to make statements about all statements whatever, including their own philosophical statements. Since this concern is wholly legitimate, there can be nothing intrinsically objectionable about self-referential statements.[2] Such statements may allow the deduction of contradictions in standard systems of logic, but it is possible, as Fitch has shown, to build restrictions into our logical rules so that these contradictions cannot be derived. The system resulting from these restrictions will differ from the usual systems in not containing, for example, the familiar law of the excluded middle; but it will still be a consistent, workable system, and it will allow a philosopher to carry on his proper job without logical interference.

It might appear bewildering to the reader to learn that there are many alternative systems of logic and that experts do not fully agree on which system is best. It may prove comforting to know, therefore, that the number of standard systems is relatively small and that there is sufficient agreement on the usefulness of these systems so that they are almost uniformly taught in the world's better colleges and universities. Departures from these standard systems are not difficult to understand, and the student soon learns why they are made. In general, the choice of a particular system of logic is purely practical; if a man is prepared to modify his system in the face of difficulties, he is proceeding as reasonably as can be expected.

Before concluding this discussion it may be helpful to list some generally accepted logical rules in order to provide a better picture of the relation between logical rules and logical truths. The rules to be listed fall into two groups.* The first concern the implications of basic logical words such as "and," "or," and "If . . . , then . . .":

(1) From a premise of the form "*P* and *Q*" one may infer "*Q*."

(2) From a premise of the form "*P*" one may infer "*P* or *Q*."

(3) From premises of the form "*P* or *Q*" and "not-*P*" one may infer "*Q*."

(4) From premises of the form "*P*" and "If *P*, then *Q*" one may infer "*Q*."

The second group of rules provides means of obtaining logical truths—such truths being, for the pragmatist, statements that are assertible purely on logical grounds. The following are two familiar rules of this kind:

(5) If a conclusion "*C*" may be inferred from a premise "*P*" by logical rules of inference, then the conditional statement "If *P*, then *C*" may be asserted on purely logical grounds (it is logically true).

(6) If an explicit contradiction may be inferred from a premise "*P*" by logical rules of inference, then "not-*P*" may be asserted on purely logical grounds (it is logically true).

Rules (1)–(6) are not sufficient to yield all the truths of the standard logic of statements, but they illustrate the manner in which logical truths may be generated from logical rules. As an example of how this can be done, consider the simple logical truth "If *P* and *Q*, then *P*." By rule (1), we know that we may infer "*P*" from "*P* and *Q*." Given this, we may employ rule (5) and, with the help of rule (4), infer that "If *P* and *Q*, then *P*" may be asserted on purely logical grounds, that is, that it is logically true. We need rule (4) to obtain our conclusions from rules (1) and (5).

These brief remarks illustrate the sense in which logical truths

---

* These rules will all be expressed informally. A more exact formulation of them would require certain qualifications, particularly in the cases of (5) and (6), where the reference to "logical rules of inference" would have to be made explicit.

are, for the pragmatist, derivative from logical rules. Since logical rules are accepted as a matter of convention, the sense in which logical truths may be said to be true "by convention" should also be understandable, at least in a general way.* We may now consider the bearing of this conception of logical truth on the pragmatist's general conception of a priori knowledge.

Not all philosophers who call themselves pragmatists would endorse the account of logical truth just given, but those who do will assent to the following claim: If you know which of the words you use are logical words and if you have a definite conception of your meaning when you use such words, you will be able to recognize certain statements as logically true. If, moreover, you are sufficiently clear about the meaning of your nonlogical words such as "prince" or "bachelor," you will be able to recognize some of your statements as analytic (in the sense explained on page 108). Since an acceptable definition of a nonlogical word is acceptable by convention (either your own or that of your community) the statements you accept as analytically true may also be said to be "true by convention." You may, of course, discover good reason to change your conventions, and so you cannot say that the statements you now regard as analytically true will never have to be rejected. But you can at least identify a large class of statements that, according to your conception of their meaning, are true by convention.

The question that now arises is "Are analytically true statements the *only* statements true by convention?" Since the notion of an analytic truth is ultimately based on the idea of a logical truth, which in turn is based on the idea of a logical word, we can offer a definite answer to this question only if we can draw a clear dis-

---

* A standard rationalist objection to this claim is that although it may be a matter of convention that we adopt certain logical rules, there is nothing conventional about the fact that certain statements necessarily follow from these rules. The objection is misplaced because we can make sense of a statement *following* from a system of rules only by reference to a higher-order system of rules. Since ultimately we are free to adopt the higher-order rules of our choice, ultimately we are free to allow or to disallow a given proof that certain statements necessarily follow from a particular system of rules. We must remember that what is provable a priori always depends on some system of rules and that no system of rules is ever forced upon us, however high-level it may be.

tinction between words that are logical and words that are not. But can we do this? Can we show that logical words differ sharply from words of other kinds? The pragmatist's answer is "No." As a matter of custom and logical tradition, we do, he will grant, regard certain words as logical and certain words (such as "red") as nonlogical or "descriptive." But there are countless borderline cases where we have no compelling reason to classify them either way. For such cases, a nonarbitrary classification as either logical or nonlogical is simply impossible to draw.

Obviously, the last contention is explosive in its consequences. If there is, in fact, no general, nonarbitrary means of distinguishing a logical from a nonlogical word, then any sharp distinction between analytic and synthetic truths will be arbitrary at best. This will mean that the kind of distinction between analytic and synthetic truths insisted upon by empiricists cannot be drawn. It is important to see this point clearly. If we assume a sharp distinction between logical and nonlogical words, we can then distinguish analytic from synthetic truths in the manner shown above. But if the distinction between logical and nonlogical words cannot be drawn in any strict, definite way, then our definition of an analytic truth will not, in any strict, definite way, distinguish those truths from truths of other kinds.

Pragmatists doubtful of a sharp analytic-synthetic distinction have been attacked on the ground that although we may not be able to give clear definitions of logical and nonlogical words, we can nevertheless recognize clear cases of them and that our ability to do so shows that a distinction exists even though we might not be able to pin it down. To this charge the pragmatist replies that our ability to recognize such cases does not even suggest that there is a *sharp* distinction between the logical and nonlogical; the distinction (assuming that it exists) seems, at best, one of degree, like that between being bald and having a normal head of hair. If this is indeed so, we shall not have two neat categories, the analytic and the synthetic; rather, we shall have a continuum of cases, where for many we can say only that they are more or less analytic (or synthetic) than certain others. The fact that, at best, we can expect a continuum here is not trivial, for it completely undermines the simple empiricist contention that every true statement is either analytic and concerns merely the relations between ideas of synthetic and concerns matter of fact and existence.

The importance of this skeptical approach to a sharp analytic-synthetic distinction is perhaps best illustrated by reference to mathematical truth. Thus far, little has been said in this book about the status of mathematics. Since the views of rationalists, empiricists, and pragmatists differ significantly on this fundamental topic, a brief discussion of the basic points at issue will be highly instructive at this stage of our investigation.

3. Mathematical Truth

The rationalist's distinctive approach to mathematics was disclosed in our discussion of Descartes. According to Descartes, the basic truths of mathematics are known intuitively, and others are derived from the basic ones by Cartesian deduction. The axiom "If equals are added to equals, the sums are equal" is an example of the kind of basic truth Descartes claimed to know intuitively, and the familiar laws of arithmetic such as "$2 + 2 = 4$" would count as derivative truths known by Cartesian inference from basic axioms.

In opposition to this rationalist approach, empiricists have generally argued that mathematical truths are analytic and knowable by analysis. Some empiricists, such as Mill, have admittedly held that mathematical knowledge is a posteriori and is based on our experience of counting things, but this has not been the dominant opinion. Most empiricists have agreed with the rationalists that pure mathematics such as arithmetic is known a priori by reflection. And because a basic tenet of their position is that all a priori knowledge is analytic, they have gone on to conclude that mathematical truths must be analytic.

When we consider such truths as "$2 + 2 = 4$" it is easy to see the plausibility of the idea that the truths of arithmetic are analytic. If we reflect on what is meant by the numerals of the series "1," "2," "3," "4," and so on, we might naturally conclude that they refer to an infinite series of numbers, the so-called natural numbers, whose first member is 1 and whose subsequent members are formed by a regular addition of 1. Thus, the first numerals of the series might be defined as follows:

"1" refers to the first member of the series, 1.

"2" refers to the second member of the series, $1 + 1$.

"3" refers to the third member of the series, $1 + 1 + 1$. Etc.

Given these definitions, it seems easy to demonstrate that the statement "$2 + 2 = 4$" is analytically true. Since $2 = 1 + 1$, the sum $2 + 2$ must equal $1 + 1 + 1 + 1$. But this is what 4 equals by definition. Hence, the statement "$2 + 2 = 4$" is just a special way of expressing the truth that $1 + 1 + 1 + 1 = 1 + 1 + 1 + 1$, which is an instance of the law of identity.

Readers with logical or mathematical sophistication will observe that the proof just given was very careless in its use of punctuation and that its outcome is not quite as simple as it seems to be. If "4" is defined as applying to a number formed from its predecessor by the addition of 1, where its predecessor is in turn formed from its predecessor by the addition of 1, and so on back to 1 itself, then this definition should be expressed as "$4 = (((1 + 1) + 1) + 1)$." But the properly punctuated result of replacing the definition of "2" for both "2s" in the expression "$(2 + 2)$" is "$((1 + 1) + (1 + 1))$." To prove that the two resulting expressions are equivalent we must be able to rearrange their internal parentheses. The principle that allows this is called "the associativity law for addition," and if this law is not accepted as valid we cannot employ the strategy above to prove that $2 + 2 = 4$.

It is not necessary for us to consider how obvious or how trivial this necessary law seems to be. If we are to be convinced that the laws of arithmetic are analytic, we shall, in any case, require more than a mere discussion of examples of arithmetical truths. We shall have to be shown that even such general truths of arithmetic as "No two numbers have a common successor" are analytic, and these truths have not even been implicitly demonstrated by the kind of argument just considered.

To justify the general empiricist thesis that all truths of arithmetic are analytic, philosophers and mathematicians have attempted to isolate the basic principles or axioms from which arithmetical truths are derivable and then prove that these axioms are logically true. The Italian mathematician Giuseppe Peano (1858–1932) was able to identify the basic axioms of the arithmetic of natural numbers—they are now known as "Peano's postulates"—and Bertrand Russell and A. N. Whitehead, following the German Gottlob Frege, attempted to derive these postulates from logical truths by supplying definitions of basic arithmetical terms such as "number" and "successor."

Peano's postulates may be formulated as follows:[3]

(1) 1 is a number.

(2) The successor of any number is a number.

(3) No two numbers have the same successor.

(4) 1 is not the successor of any number.

(5) If P is a property possessed by 1 and such that a number has P only if its successor has it, then every number has P.

Inspection of these postulates will disclose that they involve three key ideas: *number, 1,* and *successor.* The task of Russell and Whitehead (and Frege before them) was to find definitions of these ideas in purely logical terms. Such definitions would be necessary to prove that the five postulates of Peano are derivative from the truths of logic.

The details of the Russell-Whitehead procedure are extremely intricate. We shall merely indicate their strategy for defining the three basic ideas of Peano's postulates. The definition of the first idea, *number,* is based on the insight that the number of members a class contains is easily specified in purely logical terms, that is, without using any arithmetical notions.* If we wish to say, for example, that a given class contains exactly two members without mentioning the number 2, we can say that the class has a member x and a member y, that x is not identical with y, and that if any object z is a member of the class, z is then identical either with x or with y. In a similar way we can say that a class has any given number of members, including none at all.

Since we can specify in nonnumerical terms the number of members a class contains, we may proceed to define a certain na-

---

* This claim is qualified on pp. 127 ff.

tural number as something related to all classes of a specified membership. Thus, the number 2 could be defined as something related to all couples, the number 3 as something related to all triples, and so on. To make this approach precise we must, of course, be able to specify the relevant "something " and its relation to all like-membered classes. Russell and Whitehead found a remarkably simple means of doing this: they defined the common something (the number) simply as the class containing all the relevant like-membered classes. According to their definition, the number 2 is simply identified with the class of all couples, the number 3 is identified with the class of all triples, and so on.

To make matters easier to understand let us use the expression "index class" to refer to a class the number of whose members is describable wholly in logical terms. Given this convention, we can then say that a given natural number is the class containing all classes similar to a certain index class. The number 1 may be defined as the class containing all classes similar to one with a single member, the number 2 may be defined as the class containing all classes similar to an index class with a member x and a member y not identical with x (but no more), and so on. To get a wholly general definition of number we can say that a natural number is a class of classes similar to some index class. The relevant notion of similarity between classes can be precisely defined in terms of a member-by-member correspondence between them, an idea capable of purely logical characterization.

Assuming that the notions of 1 and number may be satisfactorily defined in purely logical terms, we may now consider the third idea fundamental to Peano's postulates, namely, that of a number's successor. If a natural number is to be understood as a class of classes, the successor of a natural number, being itself a number, must also be a class of classes. The relation between one class (or number) and it successor is easiest seen by an example. The number 3 is defined as a class of triples, which is a class of all classes similar to one with three members. The successor of 3 —namely, 4—is then the class of all quadruples, or the class of all classes similar to a class with four members. Using our notion of an index class we may therefore say that an index class adequate to define the number 4 would have exactly one more member than an index class adequate to define the number 3. This point may be generalized: N is a successor of M just when an index class for N has exactly one more member than an index for M.

To give a general, logical definition of "successor," we must introduce the notion of a *union* of two classes. The union of the classes A and B is the class of things belonging either to A or to B or to both A and B. If, for example, the class A has two members, x and y, and the class B has three members, x, z, and w, then the union of A and B will be the class containing as members x, y, z, and w; for each of the latter objects is a member either of A or B or of both A and B.

Now, let S be a class with exactly one member, that is, with a member x but no member y not identical with x. If N is a number, it is a class of classes similar to some index class I. The successor of N may then be defined as the class of classes similar to the union of I and S, provided that no members are common to I and S. To illustrate: let I be an index class for the number 5. By definition, the class I has five members. The class A has exactly one member, so that if A and I have no members in common, their union has six members. If we take the union of A and I as an index class for the successor of 5, this successor will be the class of classes similar to one with six members. But this class is just what 6 is defined as being. Hence, our general definition: If N is a number, then the *successor* of N is the class of classes whose index class is the union of N's index class and some single-membered class S, where N's index class and S have no common members.

Given these definitions of the basic notions of Peano's postulates, the five postulates can be proved to be true on the basis of standard assumptions about classes. Russell and Whitehead regarded these standard assumptions as logical truths, and they therefore argued that Peano's postulates and the arithmetical truths inferable from them had the status of derivative truths of logic, for the definitions given above will then involve purely logical notions. This position supports the empiricist's interpretation of mathematics, and philosophers accepting it have come to be known as "logicists," since they espouse a purely logical interpretation of mathematical truth.

The question whether Russell and Whitehead were successful in reducing mathematics to logic depends largely on the question whether the standard assumptions about classes needed for their proof are logical assumptions. Most of the symbols used in expressing the relevant assumptions are admitted to be logical, but there is one exception, "ε", which means "is a member of." If this symbol is regarded as logical, then the axioms of the theory of classes (also called "set theory") are logically true if they are true at all, since they do not contain descriptive words essentially. If, on the other hand, the symbol "ε" is not logical, then the most that Russell and Whitehead accomplished was a reduction of one mathematical theory to another, namely, the reduction of arithmetic and what may be developed from it to the general theory of classes.

Is it, or is it not, correct to regard the symbol "ε" as logical? According to the pragmatist, no single answer is correct; it is up to us to classify the symbol in whatever way we wish. As he sees it, Russell and Whitehead were entirely correct in arguing that mathematics is essentially the same as logic, but then logic is a great deal more like mathematics than most philosophers have thought. To appreciate the details of the pragmatist's view we must pay close attention to the basic assumptions of the theory of classes.

What, we may ask, is a class (or set) supposed to be? The natural answer—that a class is a group or aggregate of things—does not take us far, since classes in the logician's sense may be wholly lacking in members. Historically, two basic ideas have been used to pin down the technical notion of a class, one concerning the conditions under which a class may be said to exist and the other concerning the conditions under which two described classes are the same. According to the first idea, a class can be said to exist if its membership can be specified or described. If we can specify what we mean by a unicorn, we can assume the existence of the class of unicorns even though we may be uncertain whether this class does or does not have members. According to the second idea, the classes A and B are identical just when their membership is identical. If two classes have no members, they are then identical as classes since their memberships do not differ.

The first idea, that a class exists if its membership can be specified, was assumed by Frege in *Grundgesetze der Arithmetik*, which contains his attempt to reduce arithmetic to logic.[4] While the second volume of this work was still on the press, Russell discovered, however, that the idea led to contradiction.[5] This discovery prompted Frege's famous postscript: "a scientist can hardly meet with anything more undesirable than to have the foundations give way just as the work is finished."[6] Russell noted that the members of certain classes may be specified in such a way that the corresponding class must count as one of its own members and that this fact leads to contradiction.

Take, for example, the description "class that is not a member of itself." This description specifies a possible membership for a class, namely, all those classes that are not members of themselves. If we assume, as Frege did, that a class exists if its membership can be specified, we must conclude that there is a class, call it C, whose members are classes that are not members of themselves. Given the existence of this class, we may now ask whether C is a member of itself. If it is a member of itself, it has the defining characteristics of its members, which means that it is not a member of itself. Hence, under this supposition it both is and is not a member of itself. Suppose to the contrary that the class is not a member of itself. Under this supposition it then belongs to the class of things that are not members of themselves. But the latter class is C itself. Hence, under this supposition, too, it both is and is not a member of itself. From this it follows that the assumption that class C exists is contradictory. Hence, Frege's principle fails.

To avoid the inference that classes such as C exist Russell complicated his assumptions concerning the existence of classes by working out a theory of types. According to his theory, a thing A can be a member of a class B only if B is of a higher type than

A. Things of the lowest type are individuals, the next highest type includes classes of individuals, the next highest includes classes of classes of individuals, and so on. Russell's theory of types avoided Frege's troubles with such classes as C, but it brought with it further difficulties, which required further axioms. Russell's resulting system was considerably more complicated than Frege's, and other theorists have suggested alternative devices for avoiding the contradictions Russell discovered. Recent years have seen a proliferation of alternative systems of set theory, and the conditions under which a class may be said to exist have received extremely careful discussion and have been set out in various systems of axioms. At present the entire field of set theory is undergoing exciting development, and systems are being worked out that were not even dreamed of in Russell's time.

The development of set theory since the work of Frege is illuminating for the pragmatist's conception of the a priori. Whether one regards the axioms of one's favorite set theory as logical or as mathematical truths, their status is still one of "acceptable until further notice." In class theory as in logic we start out with general assumptions that we only gradually learn to formulate in precise terms. As we work with a body of assumptions, troubles also generally arise, which require us to patch up our system as best we can. In doing this there are no specific adjustments we are forced to make; we have to make adjustments somewhere, but their precise location is up to us. If, with the passage of time, certain assumptions remain trouble-free, we may gain a confidence in them that is hard to dislodge. But trouble may nevertheless arise that will require us to revise them thoroughly. The rationalist idea that some of our assumptions are self-evident is therefore, according to the pragmatist, a naïve illusion decisively refuted by the history of thought. The strength of our belief and our inability to doubt are little more than a symptom of our present state of mind; they can offer no certain guide to further difficulties that, at the moment, we cannot even envision.

STUDY QUESTIONS

1. Explain the grounds for the pragmatist's charge that the rationalist and empiricist positions on the a priori are, fundamentally, the same.

2. Explain what is meant by calling "logical implication" a formal relation.

3. Some philosophers have claimed that the notion of an adequate definition cannot help to clarify the notion of analytic truth because the adequacy of a definition is generally determined by reference to what is considered analytically true. To determine, for example, whether "royal son" adequately defines "prince" we must evidently determine whether a boy could *possibly* be a royal son without being a prince, and vice versa. Yet the word "possibly" in the last sentence seems to refer to what might, on *analytic* grounds, be true. If this is so, the objection above is very serious. Discuss the nature of an adequate definition and evaluate the merits of the objection in question.

4. Explain the final definition of analytic truth given in the text, explaining the extent to which it may be regarded as an improvement upon Kant's definition in his *Prolegomena*.

5. Traditionally, it has been argued that the law of contradiction is presupposed by all rational thought and therefore cannot be criticized on rational grounds. What is the basis for this argument? Is the argument tenable?

6. Explain in detail the counterinstances given in the text to three of the traditional "laws of thought." Do the counterinstances prove that the laws are invalid? Discuss.

7. How does the following claim relate to the views of rationalists and empiricists on a priori knowledge: "It is only relative to other logical principles that the law of identity even makes sense"?

8. Explain in detail the pragmatist claim that logic is not properly the theory of a special abstract subject matter but rather the "ethics of belief." How is this claim defended?

9. Assess the significance of the claim that there is, in fact, no general, nonarbitrary means of distinguishing a logical from a nonlogical word.

10. How, in general outline, have empiricists attempted to prove that *all* the truths of arithmetic are analytic?

11. How does the pragmatist view the status of the axioms of set theory? How does his view in this matter illuminate his conception of so-called a priori knowledge?

SUGGESTIONS FOR FURTHER READING

A clear, readable introduction to the thought of Peirce, James, and Dewey is Edward C. Moore, *American Pragmatism: Peirce, James, and Dewey* (New York: Columbia University Press, 1961). A fine paperback anthology containing extensive selections from the writings of leading pragmatists from Peirce to the present, is Amelie Rorty, *Pragmatic Philosophy* (Garden City, N.Y.: Anchor Books, 1966). The student who wishes to pursue his study of pragmatism could do no better than to begin with this excellent collection.

Most of Peirce's published writings appear in *The Collected Papers of Charles Sanders Peirce*, Charles Hartshorne and Paul Weiss, eds., Vols. 1–6; Arthur Burks, ed., Vols. 6–8 (Cambridge, Mass.: Harvard University Press, 1931–1962). A useful collection of Peirce's papers, containing material not included in Rorty, *op. cit.*, is Philip Weiner, ed., *Values in a Universe of Chance* (Garden City, N.Y.: Anchor Books, 1958). Although James and Dewey are best known to the public for their pragmatism, as philosophers neither is in a class with Peirce. Some of James' best known papers are collected in James, *Essays in Pragmatism*, Alburey Castell, ed. (New York: Hafner, 1951). Dewey's most important contribution to theory of knowledge is *Experience and Nature* (New York: Dover, 1958). Further bibliographical data on James and Dewey may be found in Rorty, *op. cit.*

The definition of analytic truth in terms of logical truth and adequate definitions is defended by Gottlob Frege in *The Foundations of Arithmetic*, J. L. Austin, tr. (New York: Harper Torchbooks, 1960), pp. 3 f. The definition of a logical truth as a true statement containing essentially only logical words is advanced by W. V. O. Quine in "Two Dogmas of Empiricism," in Quine, *From a Logical Point of View* (Cambridge, Mass.: Harvard University Press, 1953), pp. 28–146.

Quine's essay "Two Dogmas of Empiricism," *op. cit.*, is perhaps the most famous source of recent doubts concerning the tenability of the analytic-synthetic distinction. Quine's doubts are expanded in a later paper of great elegance, "Carnap on Logical Truth," in Quine, *The Ways of Paradox* (New York: Random House, 1966), pp. 100–125. Although no problems were mentioned in the text concerning the notion of an adequate definition, Quine's treatment of analyticity is partly based on such problems. A well-known attempt to meet Quine's criticism is H. P. Grice and P. F. Strawson, "In Defense of Dogma," *Philosophical Review*, LXV (1956), 141–158; reprinted with omissions in Ernest Nagel and Richard M. Brandt, eds., *Meaning and Knowledge: Systematic Readings in Epistemology* (New York: Harcourt, Brace & World, 1965), pp. 246–254. An exhaustive bibliography concerned with the analytic-synthetic distinction may be found in Paul Edwards and Arthur Pap, eds., *A Modern Introduction to Philosophy*, 2nd ed. (New York: Free Press, 1965), pp. 669–671.

An influential conception of logical truths not discussed in this text is that they are "tautologies," capable of proof by a device called "truth tables." The first important statement of this conception was made by Ludwig Wittgenstein in *Tractatus-Logico-Philosophicus*, newly translated by D. F. Pears and B. F. McGuinness (London: Routledge & Kegan Paul, 1962). An elementary presentation of the truth-table method of demonstrating certain logical truths may be found in Irving M. Copi, *Introduction to Logic*, 2nd ed. (New York: Macmillan, 1961), pp. 253–273. A more advanced presentation, showing how the truth-table method may be validated by formal rules of inference, is given in Donald Kalish and Richard Montague, *Logic: Techniques of Formal Reasoning* (New York: Harcourt, Brace & World, 1964), pp. 73–77.

The view that statements about nonexistent beings such as Zeus are neither true nor false is expressed by Gottlob Frege in "On Sense and Nominatum," Herbert Feigl, tr., reprinted in Irving M. Copi and James A. Gould, eds., *Contemporary Readings in Logic* (New York: Macmillan, 1967), pp. 75–92. A less difficult exposition of a similar point of view is P. F. Strawson, "On Referring," *Mind*, LIX (1950), 320–344; reprinted in Copi and Gould, *op. cit.*, pp. 105–127. For replies to Strawson, see Bertrand Russell, "Mr. Strawson on Referring," in *My Philosophical Development* (London: Allen & Unwin, 1959), pp. 238–245, and also W. V. O. Quine, "Mr. Strawson and Logical Theory," *Mind*, LXIII (1953), 433–451. These last papers by Russell and Quine are reprinted, respectively, in Copi and Gould, *op. cit.*, pp. 127–132 and pp. 236–256.

Russell's theory of definite descriptions is presented nontechnically in his famous paper "On Denoting," in Russell, *Logic and Knowledge*, R. C. Marsh, ed. (London: Allen & Unwin, 1956), pp. 41–56; reprinted in Copi and Gould, *op. cit.*, pp. 93–105. Strawson, "On Referring," *op. cit.*, contains a criticism of Russell's theory; Frege, "On Sense and Nominatum," *op. cit.*, hints at an alternative theory; and Kalish and Montague, *op. cit.*, presents an alternative theory in formal detail.

Different interpretations of the law of identity are set out in various books and articles that require familiarity with the basic ideas of mathematical logic. The student possessing this familiarity might compare the treatment of identity and proper names in the following textbooks: W. V. O. Quine, *Methods of Logic*, rev. ed. (New York: Holt, Rinehart and Winston, 1959); Irving M. Copi, *Symbolic Logic*, 3rd ed. (New York: Macmillan, 1968); and Kalish and Montague, *op. cit.* An advanced presentation of the logic of existence and quantification from a very unusual point of view is Robert Meyer and Karel Lambert, "University Free Logic and Standard Quantification Theory," *Journal of Symbolic Logic*, XXXIII (1968), 8–25. This article contains a helpful bibliography of nonstandard approaches to existence, identity, and quantification.

The pragmatic idea of logic as a normative science involving rules we freely adopt for certain purposes was first clearly expressed by C. S. Peirce; see *The Collected Papers of Charles Sanders Peirce, op. cit.*, Vol. 1, secs. 1.575–1.584, 1.591–1.615; these pages from Peirce are reprinted in Rorty, *op. cit.*, pp. 100–118. Systems of formal logic based wholly on rules of inference are called systems of "natural deduction." An elegant example of such a system appears in Kalish and Montague, *op. cit.*, and another system appears in Frederick B. Fitch, *Symbolic Logic* (New York: Ronald, 1952).

Frege's approach to mathematical truth is explained in *The Foundations of Arithmetic, op. cit.* The approach of Russell and Whitehead is described by Russell in *Introduction to Mathematical Philosophy* (London: Allen & Unwin, 1919). A useful discussion of logicism is contained in Stephan Korner, *The Philosophy of Mathematics* (New York: Harper Torchbooks, 1960), Chap. 3. An up-to-date, advanced textbook on set theory is Patrick Suppes, *Axiomatic Set Theory* (Princeton, N. J.: Van Nostrand, 1960). A popular presentation of recent developments in set theory is Paul J. Cohen and Reuben Hersh, "Non-Cantorian Set Theory," *Scientific American*, 217 (December 1967), 104–117.

In 1931 the mathematician Kurt Gödel made a profound discovery concerning the relation between mathematical truth and systems of axioms (or basic principles) such as Peano's postulates. He proved that if any system of this kind is consistent, it will always be incomplete in the sense that some mathematical truths will not be derivable from it. An excellent, nontechnical discussion of this famous result appears in Ernest Nagel and James R. Newman, *Gödel's Proof* (New York: New York University Press, 1959). A shorter version of this discussion is contained in Copi and Gould, *op. cit.*, pp. 51–71.

CHAPTER V

Pragmatism
and Empirical Knowledge

If the empiricist's distinction between analytic and synthetic truth is either arbitrary or untenable, the same must be true of his distinction between a priori and a posteriori knowledge. The pragmatist accepts this consequence, as Descartes, in effect, did before him. But where Descartes added that all genuine knowledge is attained by reflection, the pragmatist argues that it must all, in the end, be attained by trial and error. In empirical science as in logic and mathematics an absolutely certain starting point is, for him, neither available nor possible; we must ultimately create our own principles in these subjects and then try them out in the course of inquiry. If they serve their purpose in systematizing our thinking or in organizing our experience, we regard them as acceptable and commend them to our fellows; if they fail in this respect, we abandon them in favor of others. In no instance, he will insist, can we have a guarantee that a principle is bound to prove successful. The value of our intellectual tools must always be measured by their practical success. This holds in logic just as it holds in physics; the usual distinction between a priori and a posteriori forms of knowledge is, in his view, simply a mistake.

1. Pragmatism versus Empiricism

If we consider the development of human thought from the imaginative but crude forms of cave-man culture to the rarefied and mathematical forms of contemporary physics, the pragmatist's view of our knowledge is bound to seem more plausible than the stories told by Descartes and Hume. In spite of this, however, the pragmatist's approach is highly problematic. If, as he suggests, every claim to empirical knowledge is properly made in an experimental spirit of trial and error, how are we to test our ideas about the world? How are we to determine whether they succeed or fail? The empiricist's answer to this, and it is a very plausible answer, is "By observation." For him, experiment without observation is a contradiction in terms. To experiment is to try something out and to do this is to *see* whether something succeeds or fails. If we are to be certain about the results of our trials, we must therefore be certain about what we observe. Without the possibility of such nonexperimental, observational certainty, a method of trial and error could achieve no definite results and would not even make sense. In this fact, he will insist, lies the fundamental truth of empiricism.

Although it may be difficult to see how one could deny such sensible claims, the pragmatist does so vigorously; he argues that empiricism is as grossly mistaken about empirical knowledge as it is about logic and mathematics. Since his own position on empirical knowledge is, in large part, a consequence of his attempt to avoid the errors he sees in empiricism, we shall begin our discussion of his position by developing his chief objections to this traditional philosophy. After we have discussed these objections thoroughly, we shall then consider the consequences he derives from them. In this way we shall be able to appreciate the fine points of the pragmatist's positive point of view.

As we saw in Chapter III, orthodox empiricists all accept Hume's basic epistemic principles. According to these principles, our knowledge of matters of fact and existence ultimately rests on two kinds of experience: observation and memory. Observation gives us knowledge of what is now before our minds; memory gives us knowledge of what we have learned in the past. Both kinds of knowledge are indispensable for science and everyday life—not just because they assure us of what is or was present in our experience, but also because they provide the necessary premises for our basic method of a posteriori inference.

To draw an inductive conclusion we must have observed a constant conjunction between events. Without *both* observation and memory the knowledge of such conjunctions would be impossible, and this would result in the destruction of "all assurance and conviction."

According to the pragmatist, the crucial weakness of this empiricist view is shared by every theory purporting to base our knowledge on some special foundation: the certainty of the presumed foundation cannot be guaranteed or even supported. In our discussion of the pragmatist's approach to logic and mathematics we considered his objections to Cartesian intuition as a means of establishing such certainty. If we now examine the empiricist's alternative, we shall find that the foundation he recommends is similarly indefensible.

Although Hume did not question the acceptability of memory as a reliable source of knowledge, we have already seen that his strict standards of proof render it extremely questionable. The crucial difficulty is that a present memory image is logically distinguishable from anything in the past. Given this, there can be no contradiction in the idea that even the most vivid memory image does not correspond to anything that has previously occurred. If a correspondence of this kind ever exists, it cannot therefore be known a priori by demonstration. But it obviously cannot be known a posteriori either. Since the past is by definition over and done with, we cannot hope to know its character by observation. Induction is therefore the only remaining possibility. But this, too, is useless, for we can legitimately use induction (if at all) only on the assumption that memory is an acceptable source of knowledge—and this is precisely what is now in question. A proof that memory is *ever* correct cannot therefore be given by the rational methods available to us.

Since the claims of memory are admitted by empiricists to constitute a crucial part of the needed foundation for empirical knowledge, we must conclude that this alleged foundation cannot be guaranteed or even defended on strict empiricist principles. This conclusion is further supported by the fact that the claims of observation are just as questionable as those of memory, for essentially the same reasons. This fact has not generally been appreciated by philosophers, but it is easily established by a variation on the arguments already given.

Before developing the argument, we should emphasize that observation can contribute to a foundation of knowledge only if it yields true *premises* concerning observable phenomena. This is necessary because the purpose of a supposed foundation of knowledge is to supply an ultimate basis for inference—and inference consists in drawing conclusions from specified premises. In the discussion above we have called the premises generated by observation "observation claims." Some philosophers prefer to speak of such premises as beliefs or statements, but the difference in terminology is unimportant. The point to be grasped is that a man's observational experiences give rise to basic premises, and these basic premises constitute an essential part of the alleged foundation of his empirical knowledge.

If we are to accept the empiricist tenet that observation provides a secure basis for empirical knowledge, we must therefore have good grounds for believing that basic observation claims (at least when spontaneously formed and carefully considered) are *likely to be true*. But what grounds can an empiricist possibly offer for this belief? In considering this question we must keep in mind that an observation claim is one thing and an observed object (whether impression or tree) is another. If observation is to be a basic, unquestionably acceptable source of genuine knowledge, there must consequently be a *lawful relation* between these distinct things: the claim must be reliably correlated with the appropriate object; it must reliably indicate that this rather than that object is present. But the questions arise: "How can an empiricist possibly know of such a relation? How can he know if it holds in even a single instance?"

Considering the empiricist's critical principles, the answer to these questions is inevitably negative: he has no way of knowing that such a relation exists. Deduction (or demonstration) obviously cannot help him, for there is clearly no contradiction in the idea that these distinct things, the claim and its supposed object, do not occur together. Inductive generalization is equally useless, since it can be employed only on the assumption that observational knowledge is secure, which is precisely what is now called into question. Yet if neither of these basic forms of inference can establish the *general principle* that basic observation claims are reliably correlated with appropriate objects, the empiricist must admit that the acceptability of even so-called observational knowledge cannot possibly be guaranteed or even supported.

As the last point makes clear, the empiricist's predicament regarding observation is essentially the same as his predicament regarding memory. In both cases the claim that the faculty supplies us with a reliable source of knowledge implies a general statement affirming a lawful correlation between distinct things. On strict empiricist principles such general statements can be supported in only two ways: by demonstration (or deduction) and by experimental inference (or induction). Since the general statements in question are logically synthetic and concern distinct things, they cannot possibly be established by demonstration. But they cannot be known by induction either, for induction is acceptable only on the assumption that the statements are sound. Since their acceptability cannot be established in either of these ways, it follows that their acceptability cannot be established at all—at least on Hume's critical principles.

The argument just given may seem far too simple to be sound, and we should therefore consider an objection that might naturally be raised against it. The objection is that since there are numerous forms of observation (for example, sight, touch, hearing) it is not accurate to say that induction cannot possibly be used to prove the reliability of any form of observation. To use induction admittedly we must assume that some form of observation is reliable, but we do not have to assume that all forms of observation are reliable. For this reason, we may, without circularity, use the method to establish many general relations connecting basic observation claims with observed objects. The only limitation of this procedure is that we do not use induction in trying to validate the form of observation employed in establishing our premises. Apart from this, the use of induction in defending basic observation claims is wholly acceptable. In overlooking this important consideration the argument given above was simply mistaken.

The objection is correct on one point: if we assume that one form of observation is reliable, we may employ this assumption and use induction to prove that other forms are reliable. But our proof will only be as strong as our initial assumption. If this initial assumption cannot be established by either deduction or induction, then it must be, for an empiricist, an *unfounded* assumption. If this is so, however, any further assumptions inferred from it must also be unfounded. Thus, even if we could use induction without presupposing the reliability of certain forms of observation, our proof that other forms of observation do supply us with reliable knowledge would hinge on an unfounded assumption and would therefore fail in its purpose. The objection given above is thus entirely unsatisfactory. If we are asked how we know that *any* form of observation yields reliable knowledge, obviously we cannot base our answer on the assumption that some form yields reliable knowledge. If the very existence of observational knowledge is called into question, no form of observational knowledge can be assumed without begging the question.

It is crucial to realize that the argument given above applies to observation however it is conceived, not just when the observed object is said to be external to the observer's mind. Traditional empiricists such as Hume thought that what we "directly" observe are our own subjective experiences, and the argument applies just as forcefully to this conception of observation as to the more familiar conception of seeing, hearing, and smelling. It has commonly been assumed by philosophers that a mind's awareness of its own states is infallible, but this assumption is just as questionable as our everyday assumptions concerning observation.

Consider the case of a man's firm belief that he is experiencing an intense pain. Although the idea that his belief could not be false is nowadays endorsed by empiricists as well as by rationalists, it is indefensible on Hume's critical principles. The reason is simple: a belief that pain is being experienced is one thing and a feeling of pain is another. Given this undeniable difference between the belief and the pain, there can be no contradiction in the idea that a man may believe that he is in pain and yet be wrong; the supposition that such a mistake occurs is perfectly consistent. This means that the principle "If a man believes strongly that he feels pain, he cannot be wrong," is not demonstrably certain; it cannot be known to be true by deduction. Since it is logically snythetic and also general, it can be established, if at all, only by inductive generalization. But the latter form of inference (even assuming that it is justifiable) can yield only *probable* conclusions: if all observed ravens have been black, we can conclude only that all ravens are probably black; we cannot conclude that they are necessarily black. Similarly, the most that we could establish inductively about belief and pain is that if a man believes strongly that he is in pain, then he *probably* is in pain; we could not establish that he *must certainly* be in pain under these conditions.

But as our earlier argument indicates, an inductive inference faces special difficulties in the present case. If the question at issue is whether a man's convictions or honest avowals concerning his aches or pains are even likely to be true, the question cannot be answered by reference to the man's own inductions concerning his convictions and his pains.* Such an answer is illegitimate because if the truth of his beliefs and convictions regarding his current state is in question, the basis for his presumed inductions is also in question. To carry out such an induction he would have to assume that *whenever* in the past he had a strong belief that he was in pain, he really was in pain. But this assumption is precisely what is being called into question.

The reliability of introspection or of a man's convictions regarding his subjective states is therefore as questionable on strict empiricist principles as the reliability of ordinary observation; in both cases it is impossible to justify the assumption that there is a constant conjunction (or high correlation) between the convictions and the facts. If we assume Hume's critical principles,

---

* The inductions of an external observer are clearly irrelevant here, since they would presuppose at least the acceptability of ordinary observation, which we have shown to be rationally unfounded, given empiricist principles. Note that since inductive inference always requires the acceptability of memory (to use it we need knowledge of *constant* conjunctions), we can forget about induction as soon as memory is put in question.

we may also use his words and say that the assumption in question cannot possibly be "based on reason or any operation of the understanding."

In view of the tenacity with which philosophers hold to the idea that a man cannot possibly be wrong about the character of his current aches and pains, it will be useful to consider the answer a consistent empiricist would have to give to several recent means of defending the assumption. One frequent approach is to argue that the assumption must be true because it is inconceivable that it is false. If "inconceivable" means "unimaginable," the empiricist's reply should be: "The fact that you cannot imagine a man believing falsely that he feels pain is no guarantee that such a belief is true. Your inability to imagine something is merely a psychological fact about you, having very little bearing on our knowledge of matters of fact. As for myself, I have no trouble at all conceiving or imagining such a thing, and you should not have such trouble either. Since a feeling of pain is one thing and a belief or conviction quite another, there is clearly no contradiction in the idea that a man believes falsely that he is in pain. Since the idea involves no contradiction, it should be conceived with as much clarity and ease as the opposite idea that a man's beliefs that he feels pain are always true. Hence, your supposed inability to conceive or imagine a man falsely believing that he feels pain is of no significance whatever. It surely does not show us that there is anything impossible about such beliefs."

The answer just given also applies to another standard means of defending the infallibility of introspection, namely, that a man's belief that he feels pain must be true because it *makes no sense* to suppose that it might be false. The previous answer applies equally well to this defense because if, as seems obvious, a belief is one thing and a feeling of pain is quite another thing, then it should make as much sense to speak of false beliefs about one's feelings of pain as it does to speak of false beliefs about the color of snow. In both cases the beliefs are wholly consistent and equally intelligible.

A final means of defending the infallibility of beliefs about one's feelings is to argue that it is part of the very meaning of such words as "pain" that one cannot be in error in applying them to oneself. The idea is that the word "pain" does not apply to a simple sensation or feeling but rather to a feeling-to-which-one-has-an-infallible-access. If a feeling is such that one could be mistaken about it, then it is not, by definition, a pain; it is something else.

The drawbacks of this approach were pointed out in our discussion of Strawson in Chapter 3. Just as he argued that there is no logical gap between depression and depressed behavior, so it is now argued that there is no logical gap between pain and the belief that one is in pain.* The difficulty is the same in both cases: the use of such words is necessarily based on the assumption that certain distinct things are lawfully related, and such an assumption requires justification. If we cannot justify the existence of such a lawful relationship, we cannot justify the use of "pain" and "depression" in the senses just mentioned. We may well think of pain and depression as complex states involving feelings lawfully correlated with beliefs and behavior, but unless we have good reason for assuming that such states exist, we cannot rationally insist that a man's claim that he is depressed or in pain is *ever* true. The possibility of such a justification is, however, exactly what is denied by the argument given above.

Although Hume was prepared to trust his natural faculties as an acceptable source of knowledge, he did maintain that philosophical investigation into the foundations of knowledge seems capable of "destroying all assurance and conviction." As far as the rationalist program of finding indubitable units of knowledge was concerned, a program subsequently adopted by most empiricists, Hume was led to the following opinion:

> There is a species of skepticism, *antecedent* to all study and philosophy, which is much inculcated by Descartes and others as a sov-

---

* Recent empiricists have employed a similar strategy in attempting to vindicate memory. They argue that memories are *not* logically distinguishable from occurrences in the past, because a genuine memory must, as a matter of definition, truly represent at least the crucial aspects of past events. (You cannot genuinely remember your wedding if you were never married.) This strategy cannot support the empiricist position because an empiricist has no means of showing that memories of this genuine kind ever exist. To do so he would have to show that the corresponding memory impressions are correct or "genuine."

ereign preservative against error and precipitate judgment. It recommends a universal doubt not only of all our former opinions and principles but also of our very faculties—of whose veracity, they say, we must assure ourselves by a chain of reasoning deduced from some original principle, which cannot possibly be fallacious or deceitful. But neither is there any such original principle which has a prerogative above others that are self-evident and convincing; nor if there were could we advance a step beyond it but by the use of those very faculties of which we are supposed to be already diffident. The Cartesian doubt, therefore, were it ever possible to be attained by any human creature (as it plainly is not) would be entirely incurable; and no reasoning could ever bring us to a state of assurance and conviction upon any subject.[1]

As we have seen, Hume's final view appears to have been that we have an instinctive trust in our natural faculties—our senses, memory, and ability to reason—and that if we attempt to pass beyond this instinctive trust and formulate arguments to *prove* that our faculties are not deceptive, we shall end up in a hopeless skepticism.

Hume did not employ the argument we have used to question the credentials of observation. Nevertheless, he did hold that we have no guarantees regarding the reliable functioning of our senses and reason and that such guarantees are not even possible in principle. The traditional search for an indubitable foundation of knowledge is therefore totally misguided in his mature opinion. We must pursue our search for knowledge with the opinions we instinctively possess, "avoding all distant and high inquiries" and confining our thought to common life and to "such subjects as fall under daily practice and experience."[2] Our aim in life, Hume thought, is action, not esoteric understanding; our "reason is, and ought only to be, the slave of [our] passions, and can never pretend to any other office than to serve and obey them."[3]

2. *Knowledge and Its Presuppositions*

The position Hume takes in the passage above is closely related to that of the pragmatist. Like Hume, the pragmatist insists that we can have no a priori guarantee of the reliability of our senses and reason, but that we have no alternative to trusting them (at least provisionally) in our efforts to achieve our rational objectives. He also agrees with Hume that there are no indubitable first principles on which we might, following Descartes, hope to base the rest of our knowledge. In his view we must proceed with the mixture of knowledge an error we now possess, hoping to improve it in the course of critical inquiry. This approach does not require, however, that we have blind faith in the soundness of our faculties; we need assume only that they are generally sound and hold to this assumption until we encounter good reason to assume otherwise. Certainty, for the pragmatist, is not something initially given to us, on which we may confidently build. It is something to be pursued through a stubborn course of intellectual trial and error.

A basic tenet of the pragmatist's point of view is that all claims to knowledge, even those that seem virtually indubitable, are based on numerous tacit assumptions, many of which cannot possibly be validated in advance. One such assumption has, of course, just been discussed—namely, that the modes of observation such as sight, touch, and hearing are generally reliable sources of knowledge. Numerous other assumptions are, however, of equal importance in most claims to knowledge, and it will be very helpful in understanding the pragmatist's position to discuss some of these assumptions in a little detail. Those to be discussed fall into four categories: they concern (1) the nature and capabilities of observers, (2) the various means of observation, (3) the character of observable objects, and (4) the conditions favorable or unfavorable for sound observations.

Some of the obvious examples of low-level assumptions belonging to these four categories stand out sharply when we consider such cases as these:

(1) Jones claims to have seen that a certain traffic light was green.

(2) Smith claims to see a needle in a neighboring haystack.

(3) Harris claims to have observed a unicorn in his garden.

(4) Roberts claims to have seen a UFO (an unidentified flying object) while driving home on a wet, spring evening.

If Jones' claim was made in response to an allegation that he drove through a red light and thereby caused a serious accident, we would accept his claim as true only on the assumption, among others, that he was not color-blind, not dishonest, and the like. These assumptions would concern his reliability as an observer, specifically, as a color observer. Smith's claim would no doubt be rejected out of hand, even if the neighboring haystack were only a dozen feet distant. It would be ruled out on the basis of standard assumptions about needles, sight, and haystacks—for example, that needles are very small and hard to see except at very short distances and that stacked hay is a superb camouflage for them.

Harris' and Roberts' claims would probably also be rejected, at least in the absence of an enormous amount of further evidence. The assumption that unicorns are mythical beings is sufficiently well grounded to make the truth of Harris' claim virtually miraculous. The existence of UFOs is perhaps debatable, so that it may be deemed possible that Roberts saw one. On the other hand, the conditions under which his observation was allegedly made seem sufficient to reduce the possibility to an utter minimum. He was driving his car on a wet night, which means that he no doubt observed the phenomenon through a wet window on which lights from buildings and passing cars were probably reflected. Given all this, the chances that Roberts did see a UFO would seem to be virtually nil; it is far more likely that he saw something else, perhaps merely the reflection of a light on his windshield.

The assumptions brought out in these four cases involve a minimum of theory and might therefore be called "low level." But the persistent controversy between rationalists, empiricists, and pragmatists calls to mind assumptions of a more general, theoretical kind, which are also inevitably involved in the assessment of observation claims. These high-level assumptions concern the fundamental nature and structure of reality, and the acceptability of low-level assumptions is logically dependent upon them.

Consider, first, the notion of an observer. For such thinkers as Plato, St. Augustine, and Descartes, an observer is essentially a soul, spirit, or mind, which is not necessarily dependent on a physical body. The soul may use a body in perception, but it can, at least theoretically, exist disembodied. This conception of an observer was sharply attacked by Hume. He was unable to introspect the existence of such a soul or spirit, and he could think of no good reason to postulate its existence. Although from a critical point of view he regarded an observer merely as a bundle of impressions and ideas, he was prepared to accept a less exotic conception when following the dictates of instinct and common sense. According to the latter conception, an observer is presumably a rational animal, a being of flesh and blood in constant causal interaction with its physical and social environment. Observation, on this view, is a matter of sight, touch, and hearing: it involves the physical interaction of one thing with another.

Descartes, as we have seen, had a very poor estimate of the claims of observation. For him, observation is inherently deceptive, supplying us with confused ideas that do not adequately represent the world around us. Recent defenders of common sense have energetically attacked Descartes' point of view, but the deceptiveness of observation has always been stressed, oddly enough, by thinkers with profound scientific interests. According to many of the latter, the world of common sense is essentially an objective appearance. For early thinkers in this tradition, the world consists of atoms and the void: the colors we see are actually the subjective effects of the world on our nervous systems. For more recent thinkers in this tradition, the world is rather an unimaginably complex system of events in a four-dimensional continuum of space-time. For them, an observer is simply part of this system; there is no such thing as a spirit or soul that sets him apart from this natural order.

It is not necessary here, in a discussion of general theories of knowledge, to adjudicate between these rival assumptions concerning the fundamental character of reality. It is enough for our immediate purposes to note that some such fundamental assumptions must be made by systematic thinkers and that the assumptions they make will play a crucial role in determining the acceptability of their lower-level assumptions concerning observers and observed objects. Thus, one can reasonably maintain that, say, Smith is a reliable color observer only if one has some idea, however vague, of the sort of being Smith is (Is he a spirit or a rational animal?), of the sort of thing that is or can be colored (physical things or impressions?), and of the means by which colored things are observed (Are they seen or introspected?). Without assumptions of this kind, one's claim that Smith is a reliable color observer would not make definite sense, let alone be capable of being defended.

If the meaning and acceptability of an observation claim are, in this way, ultimately determined by a system of background assumptions, it follows that the certainty of such a claim is always *conditional* rather than categorical. By saying that the certainty of a claim is conditional we mean that its certainty depends on the certainty of something else. The certainty, for example, of Descartes' claim that he must exist as a "thing that thinks" was conditional because it depended on the certainty of his assumption that thinking requires a thinker. If this assumption is denied, as it was by Hume and Russell, further proof would be required that a thinking *thing* exists. Descartes drew his conclusion, we may recall, on general principles; he claimed to know that he existed before he knew what kind of "thinking thing" (whether body or mind) he was. To undermine his general principle (if this can be done) is to undermine his initial certainty in the existence of himself as a thinking "thing." This is what Russell (and even Hume) attempted to do.

The idea that the certainty of an observation claim is conditional on the certainty of a system of background assumptions is extremely important, for it thoroughly undermines the view that our empirical knowledge must rest on some basic foundation. If we must grant that the certainty of a supposed basic claim is conditional on the certainty of a system of background assumptions, then we have no alternative but to admit that such claims cannot possibly constitute an ultimate foundation on which the remainder of our knowledge rests. Far from providing this ultimate foundation, such claims are acceptable only *on the condition* that higher-level claims are acceptable—claims about perceivers, doubters, or intuiters; about perception, doubt, or intuition; and about the nature of the objects perceived, conceived, or otherwise known. Since these higher-level claims cannot themselves be inferable from the lower-level claims that presuppose them, the foundations conception of empirical knowledge must therefore be mistaken in every guise it takes.

It is important to realize that this criticism of the foundations theory applies to meaning as well as to knowledge. If, for example, an observation claim is to be evaluated by reference to high-level assumptions about observers, our very conception of an observation claim will depend on our conception of an observer and our conception of what observation is. This point was partly seen by Descartes when he insisted that the data of experience require interpretation by reference to general principles. He did not fully appreciate the point, the pragmatist would insist, because in seeking his indubitable foundation for knowledge he claimed to have a direct intuition of his existence as a thinker. Such an intuition could not be wholly direct, however, since it is based on the assumptions that thinking is necessarily the activity of a thing or "thinking substance" and that doubting is a species of thinking.

This relatively minor lapse is not, for the pragmatist, Descartes' fundamental error. His chief mistake was his assumption that the relevant principles of interpretation are necessarily true and are not subject to revision in the light of further investigation. According to the pragmatist, all our background assumptions, even those of the highest level, are subject to thoroughgoing revision and owe their acceptability to the success we have in using them to order our experience. Descartes' distinctive assumptions—for example, that thinking is the activity of an immaterial soul and that there must be as much reality or perfection in a total cause as is contained, formally or objectively, in its effect—are, in fact, rejected by most pragmatists largely on the ground that they are out of line with current assumptions that have proved more satisfactory for the interpretation of our experience and our world.

The pragmatists's contention—that our background assumptions are subject to revision in the light of scientific progress and that such revision has a crucial bearing on the meaning of even low-level observation claims—puts some of the perennial disputes about certainty in an entirely new light. If anything has seemed conclusive to the great majority of philosophers it is that we cannot possibly be in error about the fact of our own existence. Yet if we are asked "Just what do you mean by your 'self'?" we can easily see that the possibility of error here is not so remote. Descartes was convinced that selves are souls united to bodies, but today this conception hardly has a place in experimental psychology. Aristotle's conception of a self as a rational animal would seem far more acceptable to the educated layman, but even this conception would be allowed by some contemporary psychologists only with great qualification. Our commitments as to what our *self* is are therefore subject to actual as well as to merely possible controversy; thus, any presumed intuition of our own existence is not obviously and unproblematically true. This holds good even if we have only a very minimal conception of our self as an X that thinks; for what is "an X" supposed to be, and how are we to know that such Xs really do exist?

In this connection we might observe that the concept of thinking is just as vulnerable as the concept of a self. If we consider the history of thought, we shall see that the concept of thinking has been under constant development from the time of Plato to the present. Plato's conception was different from Aristotle's, Aristotle's was different from Descartes', Descartes' was different from Hume's and Kant's, Hume's and Kant's were both different from Freud's, and Freud's was very different from that of many contemporary philosophers, psychologists, and cyberneticists. If, consequently, we have anything definite in mind by the word "thinking," our claim to utter certainty in the fact of our thinking is controversial. Of course, if our conception of thinking is so vague that it is not inconsistent with any of the more definite conceptions just mentioned, our claim to utter certainty about our thinking is so vague that it is scarcely of interest, philosophical or otherwise.

As a final example of our conceptual vulnerability, consider the case of color. Philosophers confident that a skeptical view of the external world is completely unwarranted often argue that it is possible to pile up so much evidence in favor of the idea that a certain thing is, say, red that it is preposterous to suppose that one could be wrong in so describing it. For the pragmatist, this kind of claim is significantly mistaken. He will grant that as long as our present conception of color is not in question it may be wholly unreasonable to believe that we might have occasion to doubt the truth of our description. But our very concept of color is potentially just as debatable as any other empirical concept, and considerations may always arise that will require that we abandon it. If this should happen, what a man claims when he says "It is red" may be regarded as false. It may be held that in *his* sense of the word nothing in the entire universe is red; the quality is purely imaginary.

The possibility just mentioned is not entirely fanciful. The concept of color has been a source of constant debate in the history of thought, and the concept current in Aristotle's day is now considered definitely erroneous by most sophisticated thinkers. According to Aristotle, color is a continuous feature of three-dimensional bodies, and its presence in nature is not logically dependent on the peculiarities of human perceivers. Yet ever since the scientific revolution of the seventeenth century, it has been commonly held that color is, at best, a power or disposition of a natural body to stimulate perceivers in a special way. It is, of course, entirely possible that this modern conception of color is disputable or even definitely mistaken. But the concept of this quality is not intrinsically unproblematic, and it is perfectly reasonable to suppose that a given observer's conception might always be declared scientifically unacceptable.

The point illustrated by these examples may be summarized as follows. At a given stage in our intellectual or cultural development we employ concepts in making claims that, according to our current standards, are virtually unassailable. Since the background assumptions relevant to these claims are generally presumed to be sound and are not, in any case, always kept foremost in our minds, we have a tendency to assume that the possibility of our being wrong in making such claims is so remote as to be unworthy of serious consideration. But the standards and assumptions bearing on our claims are not immune to revision or even complete repudiation. If such repudiation becomes necessary in view of further theoretical development, the relevant concepts will no longer be regarded as tenable and the claims we formerly made when using them will be rejected as erroneous. It is largely in view of this possibility that the pragmatist insists that we can always be in error in making a certain claim, no matter how good our evidence might otherwise seem to be.

Before turning to the question of exactly how, according to the pragmatist, the background assumptions presupposed by low-level claims are to be justified, we should consider an important objection that is bound to arise at this point. The objection is that our high-level presuppositions could not possibly turn out to be false, because they are analytic or true by definition. If, for example, Descartes *meant* "conscious activity of a soul" when he used the word "thinking" (or *pensant*) it would then follow that if he did think, he must *be* a soul. This inference could not be rejected on empirical grounds, for it would be guaranteed by the meaning of his words. It may be that we no longer wish to use Descartes' language, but we cannot say that he was in error in what he claimed. To put the point more generally, if the high-level assumptions discussed above are guaranteed by the meaning of their basic terms, the suggestion that they may be ruled out by factual discoveries is seriously mistaken and the inference drawn by the pragmatist (that out-and-out certainty may not be attained in one's low-level claims) is mistaken as well.

Suppose we allow that Descartes may indeed have meant "conscious activity of a soul" by his use of the word "thinking." Given this supposition, we are committed to agree that if Descartes is thinking (in his sense of the word), then he must exist as a soul. The question is, though, "Did Descartes ever think in this sense?" If we believe that souls or immaterial spirits do not exist, we shall have to say "No. Since souls do not exist, there can be no conscious activities of souls either." The consequence of this for the objection just raised should be clear. If Descartes did mean what we are supposing he meant, then to assure himself that he does think, he would have to assure himself that he is a soul or spirit. Since we are assuming that souls or spirits do not exist, we may therefore continue to reject his proof of his existence as a thinking soul. Our rejection may be based, moreover, wholly on empirical grounds; even though in Descartes' sense of the word it is an analytic truth that if thinking occurs a soul must exist, it in no way follows that our objection is illegitimate or inconclusive. He was still wrong in believing that he existed as a thinking soul.

As this reply makes clear, it is immaterial to the pragmatist whether we regard high-level background assumptions as analytic or as synthetic. In his view the distinction between analytic and synthetic statements is neither sharp nor important. If we choose to call our background assumptions "analytic" rather than "synthetic," we may certainly do so—but we should not assume that this choice of terminology will significantly affect the general acceptability of these assumptions. Under either description we may be required to modify or reject them on the basis of purely factual considerations. If we call them "synthetic," such considerations may lead us to say that they were false all along; if we call them "analytic," we may be led to say that as formerly understood they did not actually apply to the world as we now know it. The result of factual discoveries may therefore be essentially the same in both cases: as formerly understood our high-level assumptions did not truly describe the objects of the word, and in thinking that they did we were in error.

3. Justification and the H-D Method

If it is immaterial to the pragmatist whether we regard our high-level assumptions as analytic or synthetic, he cannot reasonably allow that our means of justifying them may be fundamentally different from our means of justifying our basic principles of logic and mathematics. We have already seen that in his view our ultimate justification for relying on certain logical assumptions is only that they have thus far proved satisfactory in systematizing our discourse and in governing the formal inferences we are prepared to make. In his view, a similar justification is the only kind possible for our high-level assumptions about the world. If such assumptions facilitate our reasoning in our effort to work out a critically responsive, yet relatively simple, unified, and comprehensive picture of ourselves and the world, then we are entitled to accept them as a basis for further inferences—at least until something better comes along.

To any serious student of the theory of knowledge the crucial words of the last statement are, no doubt, "critically responsive." How, he will ask, are we to understand them? Is there not some special procedure we should follow in making sure that our picture of the world is indeed critically responsible? For many philosophers sympathetic to pragmatism, the answer is "Yes." In their view our high-level assumptions are frequently generated by our need to explain various lower-level facts, and our means of testing such assumptions is to derive predictions from them that we can proceed to test for accuracy. This means of testing and therefore justifying high-level assumptions has come to be known as the *"hypothetico-deductive"* (or "H-D") method, and pragmatists typically insist that we can have a satisfactory theory of knowledge only if we accept this method as a legitimate supplement to the traditional methods of deduction and induction.

A simple application of this new method may be described as follows. Suppose we believe, on the basis of a good deal of experience, that all swans are white. If we should then encounter a black swan, we should naturally be surprised and want some explanation for this curious phenomenon. It might occur to us that the swan we see is not a mutant but an instance of a local subspecies of swans, rarely found in other parts of the world. To test this hypothesis we should make some predictions. On the assumption that there really is such a local subspecies, we may infer that if we hunt for swans in this local region we shall encounter more black ones and shall find, in addition, that the young of the black ones are also black. If this prediction turns out to be satisfied, we shall then regard our hypothesis as confirmed to a certain degree. The hypothesis may still, of course, be false, for further predictions made on its basis may fail. But if all the predictions it leads us to make turn out to be true, we shall eventually regard it as highly confirmed and worthy of rational acceptance.

The basic strategy of the new method is to predict on the basis of a hypothesis that certain events will occur under specified conditions and then check these predictions for accuracy. Schematically, this strategy may be expressed as follows. If H is a hypothesis or general assumption and C is a set of conditions under which a certain result R is expected, then the forms of inference used to confirm or refute H are these:

CONFIRMATION	REFUTATION
If H and C, then R.	If H and C, then R.
C obtains.	C obtains.
R obtains.	R does not obtain.
Therefore, H is, to a degree, confirmed.	Therefore, H is refuted.

Both schemata are highly simplified, and the important notion of a *degree* of confirmation is not properly defined. The essential idea, however, is this: If predictions based on H are frequently made and if, in addition, the predicted R obtains whenever the stipulated conditions C obtain (for many different Rs and Cs), then the degree of support or confirmation for H becomes progressively higher. If, on the other hand, a predicted R fails when the conditions C clearly obtain, then the hypothesis H must be modified or rejected. The latter alternative is required by deductive logic. By the logical principle of *modus tollens*, if H and C imply R, then if R is false, the conjunction of H and C is also false. A conjunction is false, however, when at least one of its members or conjuncts is false; if C is granted to be true, it must therefore follow, solely by the laws of deductive logic, that H is false as well.

The H-D method clearly owes its name to the fact that it allows us to test a hypothesis by determining whether predictions deduced from it do, under the specified conditions, obtain. The method is, as we shall see, rather more complicated than indicated above, and recent discussion has shown that it requires some crucially important qualifications. But before considering the form that these qualifications must take, we may briefly note some of the striking advantages the method possesses—assuming, that is, that we may regard it as basically acceptable.

As we saw in Chapter III, all forms of empiricism have faced insoluble problems about the existence and nature of things we cannot directly observe. Our knowledge of the past, of other minds, and even of inanimate external objects such as trees or electrons, has been called sharply into question by consistent empiricists. Doubts about such matters are logically unavoidable for them because the objects in question are logically distinct from anything we can directly experience, and there is no way of inferring the existence of such objects from what we can experience either by deduction or by Hume's method of experimental inference. Doubts of this kind are, however, easily resolved by the use of the H-D method, and this is a fundamental reason why many pragmatists argue that the method is indispensable for an adequate theory of empirical knowledge.

Consider our presumed knowledge of past events such as Napoleon's famous coup d'état. First, the hypothesis that the man Napoleon existed early in the nineteenth century and did make himself Emperor of France by a coup d'état does explain a host of ascertained facts, such as portraits of him placing a crown on his own head, descriptions of his action in various memoirs written by his presumed contemporaries, and the like. In addition to this, however, we may use the hypothesis to make numerous predictions about what we shall probably find written about him in newly discovered memoirs and in previously unexamined archives. Predictions of this kind have, of course, been widely satisfied, for our confidence in Napoleon's existence and in his coup d'état is very great, and it is based on all sorts of historical documents, many of which were not discovered until the present century. In view of the abundant historical data on Napoleon's life and times and the extended research by professional historians in working out our current picture of him and his reign, it is irrational to doubt his past existence—even though, as empiricists insist, we have no direct means of inspecting the past.

Consider next our presumed knowledge of the feelings, thoughts, and emotions of other human beings. Again, we may admit with the empiricist that we have no direct means of inspecting the mind of another person, but the hypothesis that our fellows do think, feel, and have hopes and desires is firmly established by the countless successful predictions we can make on its basis. If we assume, for example, that there is a distinctive experience, pain, that is notably unpleasant to those having it and typically results from burns, cuts, and abrasions, we may test our assumption by predicting what a person will say or do when he is cut or burned. It is true, of course, that the success of these predictions does not logically ensure that other people feel pain, but the conspicuous success we constantly have in explaining and predicting so-called pain behavior by reference to our assumptions about pain and its typical causes certainly adds persuasive force to them.

This use of the H-D method will not, incidentally, require that we accept the doubtful assumption that each of us generates concepts of pain and the like solely from his own case and then uses the H-D method to justify a projection of these concepts to the cases of others. On the contrary, we may agree completely with Strawson that we learn psychological language from other members of our culture and that words such as "pain" and "depression" are, as a matter of social convention, taken to apply to complex states involving feelings as well as behavior. The H-D method would simply be used to justify the general assumptions on which the use of such words were shown to be based. In using "depression" in the sense discussed by Strawson, we must assume that there is a lawful relation between depressed behavior and feelings of depression. Although this assumption cannot, as we saw, be justified on strict empiricist principles, it can, no doubt, be justified by the numerous explanations it permits and the successful predictions it allows. This use of the H-D method would therefore be wholly compatible with the claim made by most contemporary philosophers, that psychological concepts arise in a social context and are applied in accordance with intersubjective rules.

As a final application of the H-D method, consider the case of scientific entities such as protons. Again, although we cannot directly observe such things, we can confirm the theory positing them by reference to various predictions it allows us to make. We can predict, for example, that if positively charged protons are passed through the gas of a Wilson cloud chamber, distinctive trails of ionized gas should then be observable. Such predictions are easily verified, and this provides some reason for accepting the theory as at least approximately true. Of course, many further tests are needed to support such a theory, and ways must be devised of ruling out plausible alternative hypotheses that would explain the facts equally well. But this kind of testing has no doubt been carried out by physicists to an adequate degree, and for this reason we are entitled to accept their word that the theory holds good. The main point for us as philosophers is not, in any case, whether or exactly how *that* theory is confirmed; it is rather that philosophical doubts about evidence cannot invalidate all theories of that type. Such doubts can be ruled out as unjustifiable by close attention to the H-D method.

4. The New Riddle of Induction

Since the H-D method promises an easy escape from so many serious philosophical problems, its credentials must be examined very carefully. Many empiricists have felt that it is too good to be true and that we are on much safer ground if we restrict ourselves to ordinary induction.* In reply to this, pragmatists commonly maintain that the H-D method is at least as good as induction and that we must employ the method if we are to establish the general reliability of memory and so use induction with at least some semblance of rationality. As we observed earlier, if the claims of memory are not in some degree justified, we could

---

* Orthodox empiricists object to the H-D method for the same reason they object to strong forms of analogical inference: it may lead to conclusions about items that are unobservable in principle. As in the case of analogy (see pp. 92 f.), they will generally allow a weakened form of the method that is applicable only to things that are observable. In such a weakened form the H-D method can, in fact, be deduced from a combination of induction and deduction. Very roughly, the deduction can be accomplished as follows. The principle to be derived is (1): If the predictions warranted by H are true in all examined instances, then H is probably true. The inductive part of the proof is (2): If the predictions warranted by H are true in all examined instances, then probably *all* predictions warranted by H are true. By deduction it can be proved that (3): Any statement that warrants only true predictions must be true. Principle (1) is then inferred from (2) and (3). Needless to say, this description of the strategy is highly simplified; principles (1) and (2) are far more complicated than they are here described.

not pretend to have the knowledge of *constant* conjunctions needed for the use of induction.

Although much ingenuity has been expended in seeking satisfactory justifications of both induction and the H-D method, the problem has been revolutionized in the past few years by a remarkably simple argument showing that both methods, as traditionally understood, are invalid and require correction by novel principles. This argument was formulated by Nelson Goodman in posing what he calls "the new riddle of induction."[4] As Goodman developed it, the new riddle demonstrates a crucial inadequacy in ordinary induction, but can easily be shown to demonstrate a similar inadequacy in the H-D method. The inadequacy or "fatal flaw" in both methods is that they allow conflicting hypotheses to be derived from the same evidence and yet can provide no means of choosing one hypothesis over the other. Since this consequence implies that both methods may generate out-and-out inconsistencies, their invalidity or inadequacy as thus far described is inescapable.

When we discussed the traditional problem of induction in Chapter II, we remarked that our confidence in an inductive conclusion depends largely on the amount of evidence we have in favor of it. In discussing the example of throwing a coin we pointed out that as we gain further evidence concerning some phenomenon, our conclusions regarding it frequently change: earlier estimates, we said, may be corrected by later ones. This kind of inconsistency between conclusions based on different amounts of evidence did not seem problematic, because we tacitly accepted the rule that, other things being equal, a conclusion based on a greater amount of evidence is preferable to one based on a lesser amount. In fact, it was on the basis of this rule that we spoke of later estimates inferred from more inclusive data as "correcting" earlier ones.

Although important problems exist regarding the amount of evidence required to make an inductive conclusion plausible, Goodman's new riddle is concerned merely with the qualitative notion of favorable evidence. Instead of using our terminology of favorable or unfavorable evidence for an inductive conclusion,

Goodman speaks of confirming or disconfirming instances of a hypothesis. We may indicate the meaning of his special terminology by saying that statements of the form "All As are B"are confirmed by the fact that this or that A *is* B and disconfirmed by the fact that one or another A is *not* B. For example, the general statement "All emeralds are green" is confirmed by the fact that certain individual emeralds are green and disconfirmed by the fact that certain emeralds are (as we may suppose) not green. Since we are confident that there are emeralds and that they are all green, we know that the general statement has numerous positive instances and we do not believe that it has any negative instances. Obviously, a confirming instance as here explained does not show that a hypothesis is true or even probable; it merely provides a unit of favorable evidence for it.

To see how a given body of evidence may add equal support to conflicting hypotheses consider the artificial predicate "grue," which, by definition, applies to things examined and found to be green and to things unexamined and not green.[5] More precisely:

A thing x is grue $=$ df. x is green and examined, or not-green and unexamined.*

Suppose, as is reasonable, that all examined emeralds have been found to be green. This finding supports the hypothesis that *all* emeralds are green. But according to the definition of "grue" given above, all examined emeralds are also grue: they have been examined and found to be green. This means that our evidence regarding emeralds also supports the hypothesis that all emeralds are grue; in fact, it supports the two hypotheses to an equal degree:

(1) All emeralds are green.
(2) All emeralds are grue.

Unfortunately, these hypotheses have incompatible consequences for all *unexamined* emeralds. As a proof of this, let E be any unexamined emerald. According to hypothesis (1), the emerald E must be green, since all emeralds are said to be of this color. But according to hypothesis (2), the emerald E must be grue,

* Goodman defines the predicate "grue" somewhat differently from this, but his strategy is essentially the same.

which means, given that it is unexamined, that it is not green. Yet no emerald can be both green and not green; the idea is contradictory. Thus, hypotheses (1) and (2) conflict, even though they are supported by the same evidence.

The bearing of this argument on inductive generalization as we described it in Chapter II should be obvious. If enough emeralds are ever examined to warrant the general conclusion that all emeralds are green, enough will be examined to warrant the conflicting conclusion that all emeralds are grue. The consequence is unavoidable because, as just shown, the same evidence will support both hypotheses to an equal degree. This completely undermines the method of inductive generalization, because any further evidence we might possibly obtain can provide no inductive basis for choosing between them.*

Turning now to the H-D method, we find that a similarly unfortunate consequence is easily derived. If we are to use this method in testing the hypothesis that all emeralds are green, we shall predict that any emerald we examine will be found to be green. Since such predictions will, as we may suppose, turn out to be successful, the hypothesis in question is thereby confirmed to an appropriate degree. But the same evidence will equally confirm the hypothesis that all emeralds are grue; for an examined grue emerald is, by definition, green. To predict, therefore, that any emerald we examine will be grue is tantamount to predicting that such emeralds will be green. Since, as we may suppose, examined emeralds will indeed be green, we may therefore conclude that the grue hypothesis is confirmed to the same degree and by the same experimental findings as the green hypothesis. Thus, the H-D method, at least as thus far described, possesses the same startling inadequacy as ordinary induction.

* It might seem that the grue hypothesis could be ruled out inductively by confirming pairs of hypotheses that are incompatible with it; for instance, (1) that only green objects emit light of kind K and (2) that even unexamined emeralds emit light of kind K. Even allowing that (2) could be satisfactorily established by inductive means, such strategies inevitably fail because any evidence inductively supporting hypothesis (1) will equally support the conflicting hypothesis (3) that only grue things emit light of kind K. This merely leaves us with a further problem of the same kind: Why prefer (1) to (3)—especially when (3) and (2) are perfectly consistent with the grue hypothesis regarding emeralds?

5. An Empiricist Strategy for Solving the New Riddle

Because, as we shall see, the modifications of the H-D method needed to resolve the Goodman paradox are fully in line with the pragmatist's general position, he has, in general, accepted the paradox as perfectly genuine and as requiring a modification of his method. The empiricist, on the other hand, has attempted to dispose of the paradox as a clever trick that does not really cast doubt on the soundness of induction. In this section we shall consider a standard empiricist attempt to dispel the paradox. The weakness of the attempt will show us how serious the paradox is, and it will also help us to appreciate the basis for the pragmatist's alternative.

The predicate "grue" is obviously both strange and artificial, and its application to our experience seems less direct than that of the predicate "green." For the empiricist, this observation is of decisive importance; the green hypothesis should be preferred to the grue hypothesis because the predicate "green" directly applies to our experience whereas "grue" does not. As he sees it, grossly artificial predicates are easily constructed that will spell trouble for any valid form of inference, but this kind of trouble is purely artificial and is of our own making. It is in direct experience that we are closest to the facts of nature; and directly experienced facts are best described by ostensive predicates, which are purely qualitative and carry no implications for what is not wholly within the focus of our attention. When we introduce contrived predicates such as "grue" we fall into difficulties precisely because we unwittingly project absent or imaginary features into what we observe. In experiencing a green emerald, for example, we do not observe a quality of non-green; yet this absent quality is smuggled into the picture by the artificial predicate "grue." If, accordingly, we avoid such artificial predicates and place our trust in ostensive predicates such as "green," conflicts of the type Goodman discusses will never arise.

The line of thought just sketched is undoubtedly very plausible, for it does appear that "grue" relates to facts not directly apparent. The suggestion that "green" differs from "grue" in applying to a quality that is wholly within the focus of experience also has an obvious plausibility, even though the idea that "green" is an ostensive predicate runs sharply counter to the pragmatist's contention that experience always requires interpretation by general background assumptions. To evaluate this means of resolving the Goodman paradox we must therefore weigh the question whether the empiricist is correct in thinking that we possess key ostensive concepts and that the predicate "green" is appreciably less complicated in meaning and more appropriate to the facts of experience than contrived predicates such as "grue."

A comment on this matter worthy of our immediate notice was made by the British philosopher R. G. Collingwood, who thought our means of classifying colors very arbitrary and no closer to the facts of experience than that of cultures differing significantly from ours. As he said:

> The ancient Greeks and Romans classified colors not as we classify them, by the qualitative differences they show according to the places they occupy in the spectrum, but by reference to something quite different from this, something connected with dazzlingness or glintingness or gleamingness or their opposites, so that a Greek will find it natural to call the sea "winelooking" as we call it blue, and a Roman will find it natural to call a swan "scarlet"—or the word we conventionally translate scarlet—as we call it white.[6]

Similar remarks have been made by other students of foreign cultures, such as Benjamin Lee Whorf, who argued that our distinctive ways of conceptualizing experience are the result of a long history of cultural development and are as artificial and contrived as any distinctively human tool.[7]

These remarks by Collingwood and others do not prove, however, that we do not have simple ostensive concepts; they prove only (if they are sound) that different aspects of experience are likely to be more or less significant for different cultures and that we are wholly unjustified in assuming a priori that our favorite concepts are shared by all rational beings. There are, nevertheless, important reasons for thinking that simple ostensive concepts are fictions and that the concept of grue is really no more complicated or artificial than that of green or blue. These reasons are best developed by reference to a distinction commonly drawn by philosophers of all schools, that between a predicate's extension and its intension.

A predicate's *extension* is the class of existing objects to which it truly applies. The class of men, for example, constitutes the extension of the predicate "man." A predicate's *intension*, on the other hand, is its meaning or significance. When two predicates have the same intension, they are called synonymous; when they have the same extension, they are called coextensive. Thus, the English "red" and the French "rouge" have the same intension because they are synonyms; the predicates "man" and "laughing anthropoid" have the same extension because, although they are not synonyms, they apply to the same class of animals. (Here we assume that "laughing" means "naturally or genetically capable of laughing.")

The claim that there are simple ostensive concepts implies that the intension of certain expressions can be established wholly by reference to their extension—that the word "red," for example, can be given meaning purely by reference to red things. This idea is, however, completely mistaken according to the pragmatist. As he sees it, one cannot possibly establish the meaning of a word in this way because indefinitely many predicates will apply to any object one may refer to, and there is no way of specifying in a nonverbal way the distinctive import of the predicate one is concerned with. Take, for example, the predicates "man" and "laughing anthropoid." Since these are coextensive, both are applicable to any man one might point out. If, therefore, one is attempting to teach someone the meaning of "man" by pointing out instances of men, each instance one points to will also be a laughing anthropoid, and there is nothing in the situation presented that will disclose the special meaning of the word "man" —the meaning that differs so significantly from that of "laughing animal," "featherless biped," and countless other expressions.

Philosophers defending the idea of ostensive concepts do not, of course, think of "man" or "laughing anthropoid" as typical examples. They have in mind predicates like "red" or "green," which seem to apply to something simple and qualitative. Yet the critical remarks above apply to these cases equally well. Whether one is concerned with a color or something quite different, the instances of any class one examines (however large it may be) will be characterized by coextensive predicates, and reference to those instances will not isolate the particular meaning appropriate to the word in question. This claim is capable of proof by reference to artificial predicates such as "red when examined by a keen observer," which will apply to every red object one points to; but it should seem plausible in view of the remark by Collingwood and the familiar fact that every red object will be distinguishable from a green object when viewed by a normal observer under good light.

The criticism developed here was underlined by Peirce when he said that the meaning of every intellectual conception relates to would-bes rather than merely to what is.[8] His point stands out clearly if we consider the question "What is the difference between a man and a laughing anthropoid?" If in answering this we could appeal only to what is (or exists), a difference between men and laughing anthropoids could not be established. Since the predicates involved are coextensive, the class of men is, as it happens, *identical* with the class of laughing anthropoids. If, however, we could appeal to possibilities or would-bes in answering the question, a fundamental difference is easily established. Take a gorilla, for example. If such an animal were able to laugh, it *would be* a laughing anthropoid that is not a man. In view of this we might say that although existing men are all laughing anthropoids and vice versa, it is nevertheless possible for a laughing anthropoid to be other than a man. This possibility (or "would-be") may be taken as proof that the predicates "man" and "laughing anthropoid" differ in meaning even though they happen to be coextensive in our world.

Peirce's contention that possibilities or would-bes are fundamental to the meaning of a word allows us to pinpoint the decisive limitation of any theory of ostensive definition. Since any ostensive procedure is necessarily restricted to what can be pointed out or examined, it cannot survey the countless possibilities or would-bes that are crucial to the meaning of a predicate and distinguish that predicate from the hordes of others that, as it happens, are coextensive with it. Such a survey of possibilities can be carried out only in language and by the use of general principles—the latter being indispensable for the *interpretation* of experience.

These considerations are fairly abstract, but a careful look at the predicate "red" bears out their implication that color words are very complicated in meaning. Note, for example, that a red object is not merely one that looks red—even to standard observers. A white object may look this way to any normal observer viewing it under a strong red light. To determine the color of a thing one must view it under standard conditions, the "light of common day." But this is not all, as the example of "grue" indicates. Consider the artificial predicate "Goodman red," which means "red if examined but black otherwise." This obviously differs significantly in meaning from the ordinary predicate "red," yet it might apply to all examined things that look red to standard observers under standard conditions. To distinguish the meaning of "red" from that of "Goodman red" we must add that red things are red whether examined or not, whereas Goodman-red things are always red if they are examined but black otherwise.

As these few points indicate, our ordinary color concepts concern would-bes as well as what is; they apply to things not merely because of the direct manner in which those things are presented in our experience but also because they *would* look such and such to standard observers *if* viewed under such and such conditions. The empiricist's contention, therefore, that predicates such as "grue" differ from ordinary predicates in not being purely qualitative and in having implications for what is not present in our experience is simply false. Both kinds of predicates are not purely qualitative, since they involve the very complicated notions of observers and conditions of observation, and both have implications for what is not immediately present in our experience. The attempt to distinguish the concepts of green and grue on the basis of complexity and direct applicability to experience is thus without foundation. This means that the empiricist's strategy in solving the Goodman paradox by reference to the simplicity and direct applicability of the ordinary concept *green* must be counted a failure.

6. The Pragmatic Theory of Experimental Inference

Having seen that the empiricist cannot successfully resolve the Goodman problem by arguing that "green" is preferable to "grue" because the latter is grossly artificial and neither ostensively definable nor directly applicable to experience, we may now consider the approach of the pragmatist. Since in his view all concepts are humanly invented, artificial tools of interpretation, he cannot reasonably object to the grue hypothesis on a priori grounds. For the pragmatist, the predicate "grue" is just another possible device for the interpretation of experience, and there is nothing intrinsically objectionable about it. If it is to be ruled out decisively in favor of some other concept such as *green*, reasons must be given for thinking that, everything considered, the latter is a better, more useful intellectual tool. Such reasons cannot, however, be given in abstraction from our current concepts, principles, and methods of investigation. We must always start with the fallible system we now possess and develop our reasons on the basis of systematic considerations.

Given this approach to the evaluation of concepts, we may legitimately allude to our current assumptions in resolving the conflict between the grue and green hypotheses. One assumption of obvious relevance concerns the nature of color. As matters now stand, grue does not count as a color, any more than red-when-examined does. This fact is not, of course, necessary; we could easily regard grue as a color if we chose to do so. The point is merely that we do, as it happens, restrict colors to qualities such as red, blue, green, and their determinate shades such as scarlet, sky blue, and kelly green.

The relevance of this point to the Goodman problem is that as long as our present means of classifying colors is not in question, the grue hypothesis will carry the implication that emeralds change color when they are examined. If all emeralds are grue, then examined emeralds are green whereas unexamined emeralds are not green. Since we may suppose that any emerald we examine existed prior to being examined, the grue hypothesis implies that such an emerald was previously nongreen but became green on being examined. According to our present means of classifying colors, this amounts to saying that such an emerald underwent a change of color on being examined. The question we must ask is whether this idea is acceptable. Should we grant that examining an emerald can be expected to result in a change of its color?

The answer seems to be "No." To examine a thing for color is merely to observe it, to view it under good conditions of illumination. Visually observing a thing is undoubtedly a complicated process, but on the physical side it involves, at least according to current theories, a certain passivity: we merely receive light that is naturally reflected from the observed object. Such a reception of light does not, moreover, do anything to the object; as we know from astronomy, we are capable of receiving light from very distant stellar objects even after they have ceased to exist. Yet if we do not physically interact with an object in visually observing it, the act of observation should not bring about a change in its physical state. Given this, emeralds that are green on examination should remain green after examination—assuming, that is, that they have not been acted on by some other entity. Since the grue hypothesis implies that such a change will occur merely because the original green thing is no longer observed, the hypothesis is incompatible with well-founded theoretical assumptions and should therefore be rejected.

This argument against the grue hypothesis is plainly a conditional one, hinging on our high-level assumptions about the causes of physical change, the nature of observation, and so on. Such assumptions are not, of course, immune to revision or even outright rejection, but a revision is not required merely because the grue hypothesis is compatible with observed facts regarding emeralds. After all, these assumptions do allow us to accommodate the observed facts, namely, that observed emeralds are green; they also have a long history of successful use in the interpretation of experience; and the grue hypothesis has, in any case, no special support that is lacking for the green hypothesis and that should make us prefer it to the latter. In short, our background assumptions still apply satisfactorily to the experienced facts about emeralds and, though they rule out the grue hypothesis as extremely unlikely, the latter hypothesis has no special support that makes these assumptions seem doubtful in turn.

The argument just given is not, of course, the only means of attacking the grue hypothesis; it may not even be the best means of attacking it. Nevertheless, it is in line with the pragmatist's approach, and it does distinguish his approach from that of the rationalist or the empiricist. Unlike the rationalist and the empiricist, the pragmatist does not reject the grue hypothesis on the ground that "grue" is an intrinsically bogus or artificial predicate; he rejects it because it has implications that conflict with high-level assumptions he has good experimental reason to trust. The pragmatist's objection is not, in other words, that "grue" is, by its very nature, unacceptable as an observation predicate; it is rather that its use conflicts with that of other predicates (in particular, with "green") that we have better reason to rely on for purposes of interpreting our experience.

If, however, the predicate "grue" and, with it, the grue hypothesis are to be ruled out by reference to high-level assumptions, the question again arises "How are these high-level assumptions justified?" The suggestion given earlier, that they may be justified by the H-D method, can no longer be accepted without qualification. As originally described, that method is capable of supporting the grue and green hypotheses equally well; so without important qualifications its use could not justify the assumptions ruling out the grue hypothesis rather than other assumptions that would support it.

If we look again at the schemata used to exhibit the logic of the H-D method, we can point to the places where it must be revised:

CONFIRMATION	REFUTATION
If H and C, then R.	If H and C, then R.
C obtains.	C obtains.
R obtains.	R does not obtain.
Therefore, H is, to a degree, confirmed.	Therefore, H is refuted.

In the schema for refutation the main qualification is that the Cs—the conditions relevant to predicting the result—must be clearly understood as involving high-level assumptions as well as anything knowable by observation. The hypothesis, for example, that all emeralds are green warrants the prediction that subsequently examined emeralds will be found to be green only on the assumption, among others, that the process of examination will not affect a thing's color. Aside from this qualification, the schema for refutation appears to hold good. There may be additional means of refuting a hypothesis, but the schema given above adequately expresses at least one standard strategy for accomplishing this.

The most extensive qualifications concern the schema for confirmation. As we know from studying the Goodman problem, whenever we have an hypothesis H that, together with acceptable assumptions C, yields a true prediction R, there will always be another hypothesis J, incompatible with H, which also yields the prediction R when C is assumed. For this reason, the schema for confirmation must be supplemented by a system of rules for choosing among conflicting hypotheses that cover the same predicted facts. The difficult question to answer is "Just what are these rules?"

To raise this question is to be faced with some of the unsolved problems of contemporary research in the methodology of science. Philosophers are now at work trying to formulate at least some of the relevant rules but the task is extremely difficult and definitive results have not yet been attained. It is, however, possible to mention some of the chief considerations relevant to any rational choice between hypotheses, even though these considerations are difficult to formulate in precise terms and to rank in order of importance. They fall under the headings of simplicity, familiarity of principle, systematic coherence, and testability.

One of the oldest maxims of scientific methodology is that we should normally prefer the simpler of two hypotheses if both cover the relevant facts equally well. This traditional maxim requires qualification, however, because the simplicity of an individual hypothesis is generally less important than the simplicity of the total system or theory that results from accepting that hypothesis. In working out his general theory of relativity, Einstein replaced the fairly simple Euclidean geometry (the kind studied in high school) with a geometry of a far more complicated structure, but the result was a gain in simplicity for the total system of physics. He clearly realized, as Rudolf Carnap has expressed it, that

> once the non-Euclidean approach was adopted, there would be an enoromus simplification of physical laws. . . . [It] would no longer be necessary to introduce new laws for the contraction of rigid bodies and the deflection of light rays; . . . [and] old laws governing the movement of physical bodies, such as the paths of planets around the sun, would be greatly simplified. Even gravitational force would, in a sense, disappear from the picture. Instead of a "force," there would only be the movement of an object along its natural "world-line," in a manner required by the non-Euclidean geometry of the space-time system.[9]

A less technical application of the consideration of simplicity is that new hypotheses should not, in general, generate puzzling facts that require special explanation, such as the fact that grue emeralds become nongreen when no longer examined. If we were to accept the grue hypothesis, we should require some explanation for this puzzling fact; yet the body of our present background assumptions makes it unlikely that such an explanation could be found.

Familiarity of principle is another leading consideration in the choice of hypotheses; and when old principles can be shown to cover new, unexplained phenomena, important theoretical progress is normally said to be achieved. An example of this is given by the early kinetic theory of gases, which allowed nineteenth-century physicists to explain thermal phenomena by reference to familiar mechanical principles. According to this theory, a volume of gas is to be understood as a cloud of elastic particles conforming to Newton's laws of motion. On the basis of this theory it was possible to derive the Boyle-Charles law relating the temperature, pressure, and volume of ideal gases as a consequence of assumptions concerning the mechanical behavior of microscopic particles. This derivation was not only a means of simplifying and systematizing a large body of theory, but in showing that familiar mechanical principles could account for apparently very diverse thermodynamic phenomena, it was hailed as greatly increasing our scientific understanding of the fundamental processes of nature.

A special case of familiarity of principle is familiarity of descriptive language. It is, in fact, essentially the latter kind of familiarity that Goodman appealed to in resolving his grue-green problem. In his view the green hypothesis is preferable to the grue hypothesis because the predicate "green" is better entrenched in our language than "grue."[10] By saying that one predicate is "better entrenched" than another, he means, roughly, that one predicate has a longer history of successful use than the other. In offering his "entrenchment" theory for resolving the grue-green problem, Goodman is relying on the pragmatic maxim that, other things being equal, we should prefer language that has proved successful in actual use to language that has not been tested in this way. Familiar tools, one might say, are preferable to unfamiliar ones, unless there is special reason to believe that new ones will allow us to do a better job.

Another important consideration is testability. In view of preceding discussion we cannot, of course, accept the empiricist's well-known principle of verification, which asserts that a hypothesis makes sense only if it is verifiable or directly testable by experience. We have already seen that any vertification by experience is acceptable only relative to the acceptability of higher-level assumptions that cannot be directly tested. Moreoover, since the indirect verification of a hypothesis can be accomplished only by the use of other principles or assumptions (many of which cannot be directly tested), we cannot convincingly speak of the indirect tests of *single* hypotheses; we must speak of indirect tests of our entire system. Even so, if a hypothesis is to be worthy of scientific consideration, its incorporation into our system must somehow make a difference for the predictions we can make; if it does not, its role in the system should be regarded with suspicion.

The last consideration is extremely important for appreciating the critical attitude required for proper scientific investigation.

As already indicated, a high-level hypothesis does not, by itself, yield predictions; rather, they are derived from a hypothesis together with a set of assumptions C. If such predictions fail, it will not then follow that the hypothesis itself must be false; what is required in this case is that either the hypothesis is false or one of the assumptions C is false. In view of this it is possible to protect a favorite hypothesis by revising or rejecting some other assumption whenever a result predicted on its basis fails to occur. Sometimes this procedure is justifiable, especially when numerous other tests have established a strong presumption in favor of a given hypothesis. But excessive reliance upon it is clearly unwarranted, for one then ceases to be critical in assenting to the hypothesis.

A simple example of how *not* to proceed in defending a hypothesis may prove instructive. Some years ago, certain members of the congregation of a suburban American church attempted to prove the existence of God by experimental means. Their approach was to place seeds in various containers of earth and to pray to God that some of the seeds would grow faster than others. As it happened, the relevant seeds apparently did grow faster than the other seeds; and this was taken as proof that the hypothesis regarding God's existence was probably true. A question for us to consider, however, is what conclusion should have been drawn if, contrary to what apparently did happen, the seeds over which the prayers were said (1) grew exactly as fast as the other seeds, (2) grew less fast than the other seeds, or (3) became blighted and hardly grew at all.

If we take seriously the logic of the H-D method, any one of these alternative outcomes should count against the existence of God *if* the stated outcome counts for His existence. Considering the identity of the investigators, we cannot, of course, easily envision them drawing this negative conclusion, whatever they might have observed. More likely than not, if the favored seeds failed to grow, they would have offered an explanation such as "God moves in mysterious ways His wonders to perform." Yet to offer this kind of explanation is to abandon the critical attitude and to indicate that one was not seriously experimenting all along. If every experimental result is to be understood as compatible with the hypothesis, the latter no longer makes a significant difference to the predictions one can make. And if this is true, no genuine testing is being done. Unlike the procedure described here, genuine testing is a risky business; one's favorite hypothesis may be ruled out rather than ruled in by the results of the test.

Each of the considerations thus far discussed—simplicity, familiarity of principle, and testability—is closely connected with the idea of systematic coherence. As we have seen, the simplicity of a hypothesis is less important than the simplicity of the total system including that hypothesis; the preference for familiar explanatory principles is partly based on the wish to increase the scope of old principles and to achieve thereby a more unified general theory; and the testability of a hypothesis was shown to involve the testability of the entire system including it. The consideration of systematic coherence has therefore been apparent at every turn in our discussion, and one might say that ultimately the other considerations are all founded upon it.

In spite of the importance of these considerations, they are nevertheless difficult to specify precisely and their relative importance is difficult to assess. Clearly, they may easily conflict in particular cases. Sometimes we must abandon familiar principles to simplify our theories (as in the case of general relativity), and sometimes we must complicate our theories to retain familiar principles that seem too good to lose. But it is easy to exaggerate the consequences of not having satisfactory general rules by which to justify such decisions. When the vague considerations of simplicity and the like are inadequate to establish a clear preference between rival hypotheses or theories, we may simply proceed with both of them in mind, hoping for additional data that will eventually resolve the conflict. The enterprise of scientific investigation is, after all, a dynamic one, and even fundamental theories are fraught with numerous subtle difficulties. Consequently, although it would undoubtedly be desirable from the philosopher's point of view to have a more exact scientific methodology, we are not in practice hampered by this lack, and scientists do not complain about it.

It may nevertheless be asked at this point: "Granted that we *do* rely on considerations such as simplicity in choosing between rival hypotheses, exactly what is our basis for doing so? Is it merely a matter of prejudice or tradition?" The pragmatist's answer to the second question is "No"; as he sees it, we rely on such considerations because they are in accordance with our ideals regarding the character of the world. At this stage of our Western culture, we think of the world as a lawfully related, humanly understandable system of which we already have considerable knowledge; and the considerations of simplicity, systematic coherence, familiarity of principle, and testability are in line with this assumption. Thus, if the universe is, in principle, humanly understandable and if, as one says, "Nature does nothing in vain," then a simpler, more manageable theory should be preferable (other things being equal) to a more complicated one. Also, if it is an organized *system* of things and events, then a unified, highly systematized theory is naturally preferable to one that is less systematized. Finally, if we already know a great deal about the nature of the world, we are not, in our present theories, completely off the track; and the concepts and principles we presently employ should not be ruled out until weighty reasons emerge for changing or abandoning them.

But given that the considerations discussed thus far are fully in line with our ideals regarding nature, what justifies these ideals? Why have them rather than the ideals of some other culture? An obvious answer is that our present ideals have proved extremely useful for scientific investigation; they have led us to the truly remarkable success of modern science. If they should fail us in the future—if, for example, the medieval view of the world as an intrinsically mysterious place should gradually begin to seem more plausible—we should, of course, proceed to revise them. But until this happens, we are entitled to approach the world as we do now. As far as our present knowledge is concerned, it seems a fortunate accident that our culture stumbled upon its theoretical ideals. They have, one might say, made Western science possible; and considering the remarkable achievements of this scientific tradition, their acceptability should be obvious.

7. The Question of Ultimate Justification

An important philosophical issue nevertheless remains to be resolved. Although, it may be granted, the experimental method just described has *thus far* proved successful as a means of gaining natural knowledge, it does not follow that it will continue to be successful. Yet unless we know that this success may be expected to continue, our continued confidence in the method is hardly justified. Is there any way in which this expected success can be guaranteed?

The pragmatist's frank answer to this question is "No." In his view we cannot possibly have a guarantee that our intellectual efforts will succeed. Past success is, as Hume saw, no guarantee of future success, and hypotheses that have proved themselves in the past may fail us in the future. This does not imply, however, that the experimental method is unjustified, for it is specifically designed to be self-correcting. When predictions fail, assumptions or hypotheses must be revised; and if predictions based on these revisions also fail, they must be revised again. There is in principle, one may grant, no end to this and therefore no guarantee that we shall ever reach assumptions or hypotheses that resist further revision. But the absence of such a guarantee does not prove that the assumptions we make *on a trial basis* are completely unjustified.

We must remember that the pragmatist is an avowed fallibilist; as he sees it, all our claims to knowledge, even those about which we have the greatest confidence, may turn out to be mistaken. But the mere possibility of a mistake is not adequate to justify a reasonable suspicion about particular cases. Such suspicion or doubt is justifiable only when we have positive evidence that something is not, or is not likely to be, true. And such positive evidence is not supplied by the mere consideration that the future may *possibly* be very different from the past.

The suggestion, therefore, that we are unjustified in making an assumption unless we know in advance that it is (or is very likely to be) true is for the pragmatist totally unacceptable—as unacceptable as the suggestion that a handy tool should never be tried unless one has a guarantee that it will prove successful for the task at hand. If we fully realize that we are making assumptions on a trial basis and that their continued use is justifiable only to the extent that they successfully serve their purpose, then our adoption of them can hardly be regarded as unreasonable. To assume otherwise is simply to reject the experimental spirit of rational investigation.

It is perhaps helpful to observe in this connection that a justifiable assumption is not, by definition, an assumption whose truth or high probability is guaranteed; it is an assumption that we are justified in making. The distinction is important, because to be justified in doing something means only that one *may* do it, that one is entitled or permitted to do it by the relevant standards. As far as accepting a hypothesis is concerned, the relevant standards are epistemic, involving the ethics of belief. To be permitted by these standards to make an assumption does not imply that one should make it or that it is bound to be successful. It requires only that one is not forbidden to make it. The assumptions we are forbidden to make by epistemic standards are those known to be false or probably false, not those that merely *may* be false—for every empirical assertion has this feature. Therefore, if we have no concrete reason for supposing that a given assumption is or is likely to be false, we *may* accept it on an experimental basis. But if we *may* accept it under these conditions, we are, by definition, *justified in accepting it* under these conditions.

As all this indicates, the pragmatist's conception of empirical knowledge is radically different from that of the rationalist or the empiricist. In spite of their dramatic differences on matters of detail, the rationalist and the empiricist are in full agreement on one fundamental point: scientific knowledge must rest on a foundation of certainty that can guarantee the truth of our most confident beliefs. For the pragmatist, a foundation of this kind can be nothing but a myth; we do not have it, cannot have it, and could not justify it if we did. Our theoretical, scientific approach to ourselves and to the world must therefore be made in a spirit that is thoroughly experimental. Lacking all intuition of ultimate certainty, we must at every stage expect surprises and revisions, advances and refutations. If our stubborn efforts yield a system of principles and assumptions that, taken together, provide more than a temporary means of organizing old experiences and accommodating new ones, we shall have achieved as much success as we can reasonably expect. The goal of our intellectual efforts cannot be a static, polished possession; it can only be further, more successful efforts of the same general kind. In science as in life it is the process, not the terminus, that should concern us—if we are wise.

STUDY QUESTIONS

1. How might one attempt to justify the claim "If the empiricist's distinction between analytic and synthetic truth is either arbitrary or untenable, the same must be true of his distinction between a priori and a posteriori knowledge"?

2. In what way does the evolution of human thought from cave-man culture to contemporary physics seem to cast doubt on the epistemologies of Descartes and Hume? (In answering, consider Descartes' and Hume's accounts of the source of human ideas and of the ultimate basis of all human knowledge.)

3. Explain the basis for the pragmatist's contention that "the claims of observation are just as dubitable as those of memory—and for essentially the same reasons."

4. "Although empiricists have generally held that a mind's awareness of its own conscious states is infallible, this opinion is incompatible with Hume's basic principles." Evaluate this charge.

5. Evaluate three recent attempts to justify the claim that a man cannot possibly be wrong about the character of his current aches and pains.

6. On what grounds does the pragmatist insist that every observation claim is based on numerous tacit assumptions, many of which cannot possibly be validated in advance? In answering this question discuss in some detail at least one example of an observation claim. Be sure to think of an example of your own.

7. Elucidate the pragmatist's contention that the certainty of an observation claim is always conditional rather than categorical.

8. According to the pragmatist, although Descartes was correct in insisting that the data of experience always require interpretation by general principles, he was seriously wrong about the epistemological status of such principles. Discuss this claim with reference to Descartes' proof of his own existence.

9. Discuss the pragmatist's assertion that progress in theoretical science may require the revision of concepts as well as of factual beliefs.

10. Why is it "immaterial to the pragmatist" whether we regard our high-level background assumptions as analytic or as synthetic?

11. What, in general terms, is the hypothetico-deductive method? What outstanding philosophical problems can be solved if this method is regarded as legitimate? How could this be done? Discuss.

12. What is Goodman's new riddle of induction? Explain how Goodman's argument applies both to the H-D method and to inductive generalization.

13. What is the pragmatist's argument against purely ostensive concepts? What are his grounds for denying that the artificial concept *grue* differs from the ordinary concept *green* in not being purely qualitative and having implications for what is not present in our experience?

14. On what grounds might the pragmatist prefer the green hypothesis to the rival grue hypothesis? In what distinctive ways does his approach to the Goodman problem differ from that of the typical empiricist?

15. In what respects must the H-D method be modified in consequence of the Goodman problem?

16. Discuss the respective roles of simplicity, familiarity of principle, systematic coherence, and testability in cogent scientific reasoning.

17. Why must a consistent pragmatist reject the empiricist's verification theory of meaning?

18. What line of justification can the pragmatist offer for the adoption of his method of experimental inference? In what sense is this kind of justification compatible with the arguments of Hume?

SUGGESTIONS FOR FURTHER READING

An illuminating discussion of the claim that an alleged foundation for empirical knowledge must consist of premises or propositions rather than mere experiences is contained in Wilfrid Sellars, "Empiricism and the Philosophy of Mind," in Sellars, *Science, Perception, and Reality* (London: Routledge & Kegan Paul, 1964), pp. 127–196. Roderick Chisholm, in *Theory of Knowledge* (Englewood Cliffs, N.J.: Prentice-Hall, 1966), pp. 24–37, defends the view, attacked in this text, that feelings and thoughts are "self-presenting states" whose character is "directly evident" to the person having them. Norman Malcolm, in "Memory and the Past," in Malcolm, *Knowledge and Certainty: Essays and Lectures* (Englewood Cliffs, N.J.: Prentice-Hall, 1964), pp. 187–202, argues that memory claims are not logically independent of past events and that skeptical doubts about the reliability of memory are unjustified. Although Malcolm's essay is clearly and persuasively written, its logical structure is complicated and somewhat obscure; in reading it the student should try to keep two questions in mind: "What assumptions do we make in speaking of memory in the customary way?" and "What grounds can be given for accepting these assumptions as true or probable?"

The pragmatist's claim that all knowledge is based on presuppositions was emphasized by R. G. Collingwood in *An Essay on Metaphysics* (Oxford: Clarendon Press, 1940), pp. 21–57. In *The Idea of Nature* (Oxford: Clarendon Press, 1945), Collingwood showed how the basic assumptions of Western thought have changed from the time of the ancient Greeks to the early twentieth century. W. V. O. Quine, in "Two Dogmas of Empiricism," in Quine, *From a Logical Point of View* (Cambridge, Mass.: Harvard University Press, 1953), pp. 20–46, has described the close connection between background assumptions and observation claims in a highly dramatic and influential way. Further discussion of the issue can be found in Thomas S. Kuhn, *The Structure of Scientific Revolutions* (Chicago: Phoenix Books, 1962), and in Israel Scheffler, *Science and Subjectivity* (Indianapolis: Bobbs-Merrill, 1967).

The view, mentioned in this text, that the world is a complex system of events in a four-dimensional space-time continuum is defended by Bertrand Russell in *Human Knowledge: Its Scope and Limits* (London: Allen & Unwin, 1946), Pt. III, pp. 177–350. Bruce Aune, in

"Thinking," in Paul Edwards, ed., *Encyclopedia of Philosophy*, Vol. 8 (New York: Crowell-Collier & Macmillan, 1967), pp. 100–104, discusses briefly the most important conceptions of thinking from Plato to the present. Wilfrid Sellars, in "Philosophy and the Scientific Image of Man," *op. cit.*, pp. 1–40, and Bruce Aune, *Knowledge, Mind, and Nature* (New York: Random House, 1967), pp. 155–176, both discuss the notion of color and explain the scientific objections to the traditional, Aristotelian conception.

For an elementary presentation of the H-D method, see Irving M. Copi, *Introduction to Logic*, 2nd ed. (New York: Macmillan, 1961), pp. 416–473. C. S. Peirce employed what he called "the method of hypothesis" to validate beliefs about the past; see *The Collected Papers of Charles Sanders Peirce*, Charles Hartshorne and Paul Weiss, eds., Vol. 2 (1932), secs. 2.619–2.624, 2.641–2.644; Vol. 5 (1934), secs. 5.170–5.174; and Vol. 1 (1931), secs. 1.250–1.251 (Cambridge, Mass.: Harvard University Press); these passages are collected under the title "Types of Reasoning" in Amelie Rorty, ed., *Pragmatic Philosophy* (Garden City, N.Y.: Anchor Books, 1966), pp. 90–100. The use of the H-D method to justify statements about the experiences of others is defended by Wilfrid Sellars, *op. cit.*, and Bruce Aune, *Knowledge, Mind, and Nature*, *op. cit.*, Chap. 5.

A very thorough defense of the H-D method in a qualified form is given by Karl Popper in his superb books *The Logic of Scientific Discovery* (New York: Basic Books, 1959) and *Conjectures and Refutations* (New York: Basic Books, 1962). Popper calls himself a "deductivist" because he holds that the H-D method as he interprets it serves mainly to refute hypotheses by deduction rather than to prove that they are true or even probable. Popper's position is very close to that of the pragmatist described in the last section of Chapter V.

The new riddle of induction was developed by Nelson Goodman in *Fact, Fiction, and Forecast*, 2nd ed. (Indianapolis: Bobbs-Merrill, 1965). Goodman's position is helpfully discussed by Israel Scheffler in *The Anatomy of Inquiry* (New York: Knopf, 1963), Pt. III, pp. 225–326. The fact that we have a new riddle of induction—one concerned with formulating an acceptable version of the inductive principle— was also recognized by Bertrand Russell in 1944 or 1945. In describing his work at this time Russell said: "I came to the conclusion that inductive arguments, unless they are confined within the limits of common sense, will lead to false conclusions more often than to true ones," *My Philosophical Development* (London: Allen & Unwin, 1959), p. 90. Russell's conclusions were later summarized in *Human Knowledge*:

Its Scope and Limits, op. cit., where he formulated a version of the new riddle: "if an inductive argument is ever to be valid, the inductive principle must be stated with some hitherto undiscovered limitation" (p. 436).

The pragmatic theory of experimental inference is still under study and development. Useful discussion can be found in Quine, "Two Dogmas of Empiricism," *op. cit.*; in Goodman, *op. cit.*; in Russell, *Human Knowledge: Its Scope and Limits, op. cit.*, Pt. IV; in Scheffler, *The Anatomy of Inquiry, op. cit.*; and in Popper, *The Logic of Scientific Discovery, op. cit.*, and *Conjectures and Refutations, op. cit.* A useful general discussion of experimental inference containing an excellent annotated bibliography is J. J. C. Smart, *Between Science and Philosophy: An Introduction to the Philosophy of Science* (New York: Random House, 1968), pp. 175–206.

Notes

CHAPTER I   DESCARTES AND RATIONALISM

1. Plato, *Cratylus*, 401; see *The Dialogues of Plato*, Benjamin Jowett, tr., Vol. I (New York: Random House, 1937), p. 190. The translation of Plato's sentence occurring in this text is by John Mansley Robinson; see his *An Introduction to Early Greek Philosophy* (Boston: Houghton Mifflin, 1968), pp. 90 f.
2. John Mansley Robinson, *op. cit.*, p. 60.
3. This famous remark is attributed to Alfred North Whitehead.
4. René Descartes, *Meditations on First Philosophy*, in *Essential Works of Descartes*, Lowell Bair, tr. (New York: Bantam Books, 1961), pp. 59 f.
5. *Ibid.*, p. 60.
6. *Ibid.*, pp. 62 f.
7. *Ibid.*, p. 64.
8. *Ibid.*, p. 65.
9. *Ibid.*, p. 71.
10. René Descartes, *The Principles of Philosophy*, in *The Philosophical Works of Descartes*, Elizabeth S. Haldane and G. R. T. Ross, trs., Vol. 1 (New York: Dover, 1955), p. 237.
11. *Meditations on First Philosophy*, in *Essential Works of Descartes*, *op. cit.*, pp. 67 f.
12. *Discourse on Method*, in *Essential Works of Descartes*, p. 12.
13. Descartes, *Rules for the Direction of the Mind*, in Haldane and Ross, trs., *op. cit.*, pp. 7 f.
14. *Ibid.*
15. *Essential Works of Descartes*, op. cit., p. 72.
16. *Ibid.*
17. *Ibid.*
18. *Ibid.*, p. 73.
19. *Ibid.*, pp. 73 f.
20. *Ibid.*, p. 74.
21. *Ibid.*, pp. 74 ff.
22. *Ibid.*, p. 77.
23. *Ibid.*, pp. 83 f.
24. *Ibid.*, p. 85.
25. *Ibid.*, p. 87.
26. *Ibid.*, pp. 88 f.
27. *Ibid.*, p. 61.

28. *Ibid.*, p. 78.
29. See *Discourse on Method*, in *Essential Works of Descartes*, p. 11.

CHAPTER II   HUME AND EMPIRICISM

1. David Hume, *A Treatise of Human Nature*, L. A. Selby-Bigge, ed. (Oxford: Clarendon Press, 1888), p. xx. The spelling and punctuation of all passages from Hume cited in this chapter have been changed to conform to current standards. Page references in these notes are to the Selby-Bigge editions, which contain Hume's writings in their original form.
2. David Hume, *An Enquiry Concerning Human Understanding*, in Hume, *Enquiries Concerning Human Understanding and Concerning the Principles of Morals*, L. A. Selby-Bigge, ed., 2nd ed. (Oxford: Clarendon Press, 1902), p. 17.
3. See Hume, *Enquiries, op. cit.*, p. 19.
4. *Ibid.*, p. 22.
5. See *ibid.*, pp. 26 f., 36.
6. *Ibid.*, p. 25.
7. Immanuel Kant, *Prolegomena to Any Future Metaphysics*, Lewis White Beck, ed. (Indianapolis: Library of Liberal Arts, 1950), pp. 14–20.
8. Hume, *Treatise, op. cit.*, p. 70, where Hume adds that the first of these relations are "discoverable at first sight, and fall more properly under the province of intuition than demonstration."
9. Hume, *Enquiries, op. cit.*, p. 35.
10. See *ibid.*, pp. 26 f.
11. See *ibid.*, pp. 27–30.
12. See *ibid.*, pp. 35 f.
13. *Ibid.*, p. 152.
14. See *ibid.*
15. See *ibid.*, pp. 152 f.
16. See *ibid.*, p. 153.
17. See Hume, *Treatise, op. cit.*, p. 252.
18. See Hume, *Enquiries, op. cit.*, p. 160.

CHAPTER III   CONTEMPORARY EMPIRICISM

1. See David Hume, *A Treatise of Human Nature*, L. A. Selby-Bigge, ed. (Oxford: Clarendon Press, 1888), pp. 187–218. For a superb critical exposition of this aspect of Hume's philosophy, see H. H. Price, *Hume's Theory of the External World* (Oxford: Clarendon Press, 1940).
2. Mill uses this famous phrase in *An Examination of Sir William Hamilton's Philosophy*, Vol. 1 (New York: Holt, 1874), p. 238.
3. P. F. Strawson, *Individuals* (London: Methuen, 1959), p. 109.

CHAPTER IV   PRAGMATISM AND A PRIORI KNOWLEDGE

1. See W. V. O. Quine, "Two Dogmas of Empiricism," in Quine, *From a Logical Point of View* (Cambridge, Mass.: Harvard University Press, 1953), pp. 20–46.
2. See Frederick B. Fitch, *Symbolic Logic* (New York: Ronald, 1952), pp. 217–225. These pages are reprinted in Irving M. Copi and James A. Gould, eds., *Contemporary Readings in Logical Theory* (New York: Macmillan, 1967), pp. 154–160.
3. Peano's postulates were first set out in his *Arithmetices Principia, Nova Methodo Exposita* (Turin, 1889). Selections from this work are included in Jean van Heijenoort, ed. and tr., *From Frege to Gödel: A Source Book in Mathematical Logic, 1879–1931* (Cambridge, Mass.: Harvard University Press, 1967), pp. 83–97. The formulation of the postulates given in this text is discussed in William and Martha Kneale, *The Development of Logic* (Oxford: Clarendon Press, 1962), p. 473.
4. Frege's *Grundgesetze der Arithmetik, Begriffsschriftlich Abgeleitet*, Vol. 1 (Jena, 1893) and Vol. 2 (Jena, 1903) is partially translated in Montgonery Furth, ed. and tr., *The Basic Laws of Arithmetic: Exposition of the System* (Berkeley and Los Angeles: University of California Press, 1964).
5. A translation of Russell's letter to Frege announcing the contradiction is included in Jan van Heijenoort, *op. cit.*, pp. 125 f.
6. See Furth, *op. cit.*, p. 127. The translation given in this text is that found in William and Martha Kneale, *op. cit.*, p. 652.

CHAPTER V   PRAGMATISM AND EMPIRICAL KNOWLEDGE

1. David Hume, *Enquiries Concerning Human Understanding and Concerning the Principles of Morals*, L. A. Selby-Bigge, ed., 2nd ed. (Oxford: Clarendon Press, 1902), pp. 149f.
2. *Ibid.*, p. 162.
3. David Hume, *A Treatise of Human Nature*, L. A. Selby-Bigge, ed. (Oxford: Clarendon Press, 1888), p. 415.
4. See Nelson Goodman, *Fact, Fiction, and Forecast*, 2nd ed. (Indianapolis: Bobbs-Merrill, 1965), pp. 59–83.
5. *Ibid.*, p. 74.
6. R. G. Collingwood, *An Essay on Metaphysics* (Oxford: Clarendon Press, 1940), p. 195.
7. See Benjamin Lee Whorf, *Language, Thought, and Reality*, John B. Carroll, ed. (New York: Wiley, 1956).
8. See *The Collected Papers of Charles Sanders Peirce*, Charles Hartshorne and Paul Weiss, eds., Vol. 5 (Cambridge, Mass.: Harvard University

Press, 1934), secs. 5.464–5.468, 5.470–5.490, 5.492–5.494. This material is reprinted in Amelie Rorty, ed., *Pragmatic Philosophy* (Garden City, N.Y.: Anchor Books, 1966), pp. 29–47.

9. Rudolf Carnap, *Philosophical Foundations of Physics* (New York: Basic Books, 1966), p. 164.

10. Goodman, *op. cit.*, p. 94.

Index

ABOUT THE AUTHOR

BRUCE AUNE was born in 1933 and attended the University of Minnesota, where he received his Ph.D. in 1960. He has taught at Oberlin College and the University of Pittsburgh; in 1966 he joined the faculty of the University of Massachusetts as Head of the Department of Philosophy. Professor Aune has been awarded two Charles E. Merrill Fellowships, a John Simon Guggenheim Fellowship and a grant from the National Science Foundation. He is the author of *Knowledge, Mind, and Nature* (Random House, 1967) and a contributor to *Philosophy in America, Matter, Mind, and Method,* and *The Encyclopedia of Philosophy.* He has also published widely in philosophy journals, including *Mind, Philosophical Quarterly, Philosophical Review,* and *The Journal of Philosophy.*